KHMER

MYTHOLOGY

Vittorio Roveda

Thames and Hudson

ACKNOWLEDGMENTS

I owe a particular debt of gratitude to Narisa Chakrabongse and Supadee Ruangsakvichit for their painstaking care and dynamism in making this book possible. Special thanks to Tom White and Celine Gauld for their critical reading of the manuscript, and to Michael Freeman and Jaroslav Poncar who made their excellent photographs available, allowing me to supplement the gaps that unfavourable field conditions created in my efforts to illustrate the text.

I wish to thank Elizabeth Moore and Tonia Tribe from the School of Oriental and African Studies, London, for their continuous support and advice, as well as Natalie Rodriguez from the Ecole française d'Extreme Orient, Paris, for her assistance in picture research.

I wish to gratefully acknowledge the encouragement of Azedine Beschaouch, Representative of the Director-General for Culture of UNESCO (Paris), who greatly supported and facilitated my field work in Cambodia, as well as Sebastien Cavalier (UNESCO, Phnom Penh), and Jean-Christophe Simon of the Conservation d'Angkor (Siem Reap). A special thank you to Dr. Augusto Forti, Advisor to the Director General of UNESCO (Paris) for insights and ideas. Finally, my thanks to the Cambodians from Siem Reap for their amicable assistance and hospitality.

First published in Great Britain in 1997 by
Thames and Hudson Ltd, London.

A River Books Production.
Copyright collective work © River Books, 1997.
Copyright text © Vittorio Roveda 1997.
Copyright photographs © Vittorio Roveda, Michael Freeman, Jaroslav Poncar.
(except where indicated otherwise)

British Library Cataloguing-in-Publication Data.
A catalogue record for this book is available from the British Library.

ISBN: 0-500-97459-4

Editor and Publisher Narisa Chakrabongse
Design Supadee Ruangsakvichit
Production Supervision Paisarn Piemmettawat

Printed and bound in Thailand by Amarin Printing and Publishing Public Co., Ltd.

CONTENTS

INTRODUCTION
Geography 7
Discovery 7
History 8
Inscriptions 9
The Angkorean Kings 9
Local Beliefs and Animism 14
Religion 14
Khmer Art and Architecture 19
Function of Reliefs 21
The Narrative of the Sculptural Reliefs 24
Women in Khmer Art and Society 24

MYTHS AND LEGENDS
The Sources 29
The Legend of Rama (Ramayana) 31
The Krishna myths 42
Shiva Myths 50
Indra Myths 53
Other Hindu Myths 54
Buddhist Myths 59
Historic Events 66
Mythological Motifs 75

INDEX OF LOCATIONS
Bakong 82
Banteay Srei 83
Bapuon 92
Phnom Chisor 97
Angkor Wat 100
Banteay Samre 126
Thommanon and Chau Say Tevoda 130
Bayon 131
Preah Khan and Ta Prohm 151
Banteay Chhmar 152
Terraces of the Elephants and Leper King 154
Banteay Kdei 155
Ta Nei 157
Neak Pean 158
Preah Palilay 160
Preah Pithu 162
Wat Nokor 165
Ta Prohm of Bati 167

BIBLIOGRAPHY 168

GLOSSARY 172

INDEX 176

PREFACE

From the first time I saw the Khmer reliefs carved by anonymous artists between the 8th and 13th centuries AD, I was amazed by their artistry intrigued by their complexity, and became determined to study them further. This book is my attempt to reveal their significance and is also the first book to present a general overview of the myths and legends brought to life in the Khmer reliefs. From the beginning I was astonished by how clearly the reliefs consitute a lexicon of signs, symbols and images offering insights into the complex cultural framework of medieval Cambodia. The transformation of Hindu myths in the hands of the Khmers, their choice of events from ancient Indian epics, the characterisation of the various actors – all are revealing of how the Khmers perceived the world.

Another element that fascinates me is the autonomy and uniqueness of the iconography in a country, which, although influenced by Indian culture, has created its own art language. The reliefs have a 'Khmerness' that makes them distinguishable from any reliefs from any other civilisation. The humour of the narratives from Bapuon, the abstract clearness of the Angkor Wat 'Churning of the Ocean of Milk' and of the 'Historic Procession', the ornate dynamism of the 'Battle of Lanka' – to mention a few – have no parallels in contemporaneous Indian, Middle Eastern or European reliefs.

It is unfortunate that I could not study in detail the reliefs from certain temples in the Kulen area and those of Banteay Chhmar, so important for Buddhist iconography. This will have to await a time when the political situation will allow free exploration of the sites. In addition, although in its heyday the Khmer empire was considerably more extensive and reliefs remain to be studied in Thailand and Laos, for the purposes of this book, my research has had to be confined to reliefs from Cambodia itself.

Another problem has been illustrations and the picture quality is not always consistent. Unlike a more general book, where the beauty of the photograph is the most important consideration, in this book rare and interesting iconography, illustrating a particularly unusual myth, has been included even when the photograph has had to come from an old black and white, or been taken at an unfortunate angle. I hope that the reader will forgive such shortcomings and that I will succeed in inspiring others to enjoy and study the fascinating myths exemplified by Khmer reliefs.

Vittorio Roveda
London, 1997

Opposite: Vishnu, Prasat Kravan.

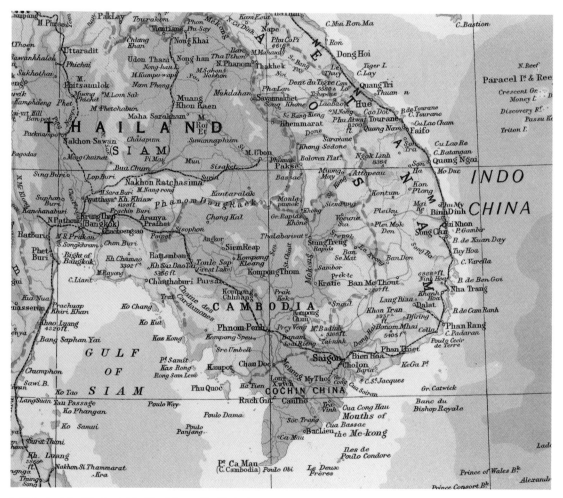

1 *Map of mainland Southeast Asia. (Royal Geographical Society)*

Introduction

GEOGRAPHY

Modern-day Cambodia is bordered by Thailand to the west, Laos to the north, Vietnam to the south and south-east, and the Gulf of Thailand to the west. However, during the heyday of the Khmer empire, centred on Angkor, its extent was much greater – as far as Burma in the west and up into north-east Thailand and parts of Laos.

Its name, Cambodia, is the English version of the French Cambodge; both are Western pronunciations of Kambuja.

Its inhabitants, the Cambodians, or Khmers, speak Khmer, which is part of the Austro-nesian language group. The modern capital is Phnom Penh, located in the south some 320 kilometres from the ancient capital of Angkor in Siem Reap province. The country's land area of 181,035 square kilometres is slightly over half the size of Vietnam.

Cambodia is surrounded by mountain ranges: the Cardamom and Elephant ranges in the west, the Dangrek range running east-west along the present boundary with Thailand, and the Vietnamese ranges to the east.

The central area is a low-lying alluvial plain where the majority of Cambodians live. Two topographical features dominate Cambodia: the Mekong River and the Tonlé Sap (Great Lake). The Mekong, which is almost five km wide in places, descends from Tibet and flows through Cambodia for 315 km. The Tonlé Sap is an immense lake 140 km (87 miles) long; it is linked to the Mekong at Phnom Penh via one of its tributaries, the Tonlé Sap river. An unusual characteristic of this river is that, during the season when the snows melt in the Himalayas (July-October), the flow of the Mekong increases greatly, it silts up in the delta region, and its waters back up. The impact of the overflow forces the Tonlé Sap river to reverse its course and feed into the Great Lake, which more than doubles its size and becomes a natural reservoir.

The climate of Cambodia is controlled by two monsoons, which set the rhythm of rural life. The north-east monsoon, cool and dry (November-March), and the south-west monsoon (May-October) which brings heavy rains and strong winds.

DISCOVERY

Khmer civilisation was almost unknown in the West before the 19th century. However, from the 7th century onwards, Chinese travellers mention Cambodian temples in their records. The most renowned account is the one by Zhou Daguan who visited Cambodia from 1296 to 1297, as a member of a Chinese embassy. He left a fascinating description of the life, customs and ceremonies of the Khmers at that time.

Three centuries later, European missionaries briefly mention the presence of abandoned cities in Cambodia. However, the first 'revelation' of the temples in the jungle came from the French naturalist Henri Mouhot who 'discovered' Angkor Wat during his mission of 1861. The emotion he felt in front of the most imposing of the Khmer temples is evident from his notes "At the sight of this temple, one feels annihilated beyond imagination; one looks, admires and, struck with awe, remains silent." His account, though impregnated with romanticism, was accurate and, completed by drawings; it was published in English in 1864. Immediately afterwards, a German geographer, Adolf Bastian, and a Scottish photographer, John Thomson visited Cambodia; the latter published his findings, bringing Khmer architecture to the attention of western scholars.

French explorers, headed by Douart de Lagrée (1823-68), and his second-in-command, Francis Garnier (1839-73), completed a scientific program and assembled their findings in a work entitled *Voyage d'exploration en Indo-Chine* that also covered locations outside the Angkor area, as far away as modern Laos. The drawings, executed by Louis Delaporte, are somewhat imaginary, as they reconstruct the temple ruins beyond the reality which could be seen.

Other Frenchmen followed, amongst whom was Etienne Aymonier (1844-1929) who began an inventory of Cambodia's monuments and the interpretation of inscriptions. Lunet de Lajonquière continued his task and published an inventory in 1902-11.

In 1898 the French founded the Ecole Française d'Extrême Orient (EFEO), to study the history, language, art and archaeology of Far East countries and established an Angkorean Conservancy in Siem Reap. French scholars devoted enormous energies to their attempt to understand Khmer civilisation; their results still remain the basis of all modern research. The role of the EFEO came to an end when the Khmer Rouge gained power in Cambodia.

UNESCO, active in Cambodia since 1989, has been given responsibility to act as co-ordinator of international aid (mainly Japanese), and of the technical, scientific, and educational aspects of work to be done on Khmer culture. It established the Angkor area as a World Heritage Site, in an effort to safeguard the future of Cambodia's past.

In the present more peaceful times, an international panel of researchers and UNESCO, together with a dynamic group of modern Cambodian scholars, are enthusiastically continuing to conduct research and deepen the knowledge of Khmer civilisation. In 1989 the Fine Arts Department of the University of Phnom Penh started a plan of training in the study and preservation of Khmer monuments.

HISTORY

Our knowledge of Khmer civilisation is based on information obtained firstly from inscriptions on stones (stele) left by many of the Khmer kings, recounting their religious and political achievements. Secondly, old Chinese texts written by travellers and ambassadorial missions contain many details, scattered through their narratives, about the Khmers. Finally, the archaeological evidence completes the picture of this remarkable civilisation, unique in the history of the region.

In the early centuries of our era, Cambodia, like other countries in Southeast Asia, emerged as a staging post along the trade route between India and China. It is not surprising, therefore, that the process of 'indianization' could easily take place. By this is meant the spreading of Indian culture in Southeast Asia, which probably started in Cambodia in the first centuries BC in the 'state of Funan' (Southern Cambodia), facing the Gulf of Thailand. It happened gradually, mainly through trading with the Southern kingdoms of India, rather than with the great empires of Northern India. The Khmer ruling class, without abandoning their own customs and traditions, selected and adopted what they needed of Indian religious and literary culture, such as Hinduism and Buddhism, together with the use of the Sanskrit language, which introduced a writing system and the first inscriptions.

Towards the end of the first millennium BC, some overlords sought acceptance of their superior status from the lesser ones by establishing central courts in important palaces, erecting sacred buildings, cultivating loyal followers, and deploying power. In this way, they created small polities or 'states', without fixed frontiers, which had, in most cases, a capital. Such centralised political and social organisations would have taken care of irrigation works, trade and warfare, and would have been used to enhance the ruler's power.

The history of the Khmer empire covers several centuries, divided into two historical periods: the Pre-Angkorean, from around the 1st century AD till the 8th century, which saw the emergence of the first polities of Funan and Chenla, and the Angkorean period, from the 9th to the 15th century, which saw the unification of Funan with Chenla, marking the beginning of the Angkorean civilisation and a shift towards a continental economy, to the disadvantage of the maritime trade of the old Funan. It corresponded with a period of the greatest social, cultural and artistic development. In the arts, it marks the decline of Indian influence and the beginning of the Khmer style; the reliefs examined here come exclusively from temples built during this period (802-1431).

INSCRIPTIONS

Many inscriptions in Sanskrit and ancient Khmer have been found within the area of the Angkorean empire, allowing us to reconstruct the history of Cambodia. About 1200 inscriptions have been found so far, mostly engraved on stone slabs. Those in Sanskrit, the language of the elite, tell of the deeds and merits of the kings, and list the temples they endowed. Information on the common people and daily life is scarce. The inscriptions in Khmer are, in most cases, a sort of inventory of the material goods of a particular personage, land and cattle ownership, lists of slaves, and of the assets of the temple. Nothing has survived of the manuscripts on palm leaves which presumably filled the so-called 'libraries' of the temples.

The inscriptions refer to a well-structured society, with each important personage having received a title from the king, or holding a designation of rank, probably not hereditary. The notion of the caste system appears to have been meaningful only for Brahmans. The rural population seem to have been closely organised around the temple's authority. There were slaves, who were taken from nearby countries and particularly from the 'barbarian' hill tribes, and were then bought and sold.

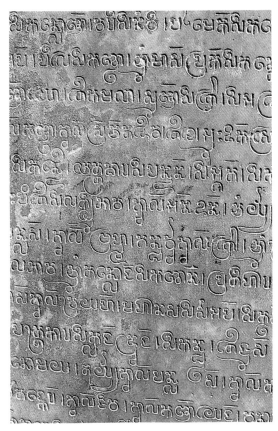

2 *Sanskrit inscription at Lolei temple, end of the 9th century.*

THE ANGKOREAN KINGS

During the Angkorean period there were 28 kings in all (see table page 12), but given the scope of this book, only some of the more important are mentioned here.

After a period of unrest, unification of Funan with Chenla was achieved by King Jayavarman II (802-835) of Chenla in the year 802, when he appointed himself *cakravartin*, universal sovereign, and reinforced the *devaraja* cult, thus putting his royal power on a solid religious base. Jayavarman seems to have spent several years in 'Java' (although probably not modern day Java) before returning to Chenla. During his rule of 50 years, he progressively asserted his authority over the Tonlé Sap region, if not over all Cambodia.

After establishing his first capital at Indrapura (whereabouts unknown) in south-central Cambodia, he moved it north, to Hariharalaya (Roluos), then to Amarendrapura (west of Angkor), then up to Mount Kulen (Mahendraparwata), where he built the first 'temple-mountain' of Khmer art (Rong Chen), resembling a step-pyramid, and designed to house the royal *linga* (phallus representing the essence of Shiva). Finally he moved back to Hariharalaya, in the Roluos area, in the northern flood plain of the Great Lake.

Two of his descendants are particularly notable. The first, Indravarman I (877-889), started an intensive building program which was to set a pattern for subsequent kings. In the Roluos area, he had a large *baray* (reservoir) constructed (Indrataka), then the temple complex of Preah Ko, dedicated to the spirits of previous kings, and a colossal temple mountain, the Bakong, for the royal *linga*.

The other important successor was Yashovarman I (889-c.900), who founded the first capital in the Angkor area. Angkor derives from the Sanskrit *nagara*, meaning holy city. It is the modern name for the complex of monuments, and the huge East Baray (measuring 7 x 1.8 km). From this time on for several centuries, the Angkorean polity, or 'state', was the largest and most important of Southeast Asia.

At Angkor, Yashovarman I built his temple-mountain on the hill of Phnom Bakheng, which was considered the geometric centre of the town. He also had the only other hills of the area crowned with temples: Phnom Krom, and Phnom Bok. In addition, he commissioned the temple of Lolei, dedicated to his ancestors, in the middle of the Indrataka *baray* at Roluos.

After Yashovarman, the capital was transferred to Koh Ker for a short time (921-944), before returning to the Angkor area (initially at Pre Rup) which remained the stable capital of Khmer kings for more than four centuries. Several major kings followed in succession, of whom the most renowned are Jayavarman IV (921-941), who dedicated to Shiva the temple of Wat Phu, in Laos, already considered a sacred

place by Jayavarman II. Under the rule of Rajendravarman (944-968), more imposing monuments were built: Baksei Chamrong, the East Mebon, Pre Rup, and the beautiful *baray* of Srah Srang. Politically he transformed the various 'kingdoms' existing in Cambodia at that time into provinces. Under Jayavarman V (968-1001) the temple of Banteay Srei was completed.

During the long rule of the important king Suryavarman I (1002-1050) Angkor was enriched with many buildings such as the temple of Ta Keo, a walled royal palace, and the small temple-mountain of Phimeanakas; he also promoted the excavation of the West Baray. In northern Cambodia he had a magnificent temple built on a promontory of the Dangrek mountains, Preah Vihear; in the south were the temples of Phnom Chisor and Wat Ek. Suryavarman I, although a follower of Shiva, was favourable to Buddhism and made donations to a monastery of this religion in Angkor. His posthumous name was unusual: 'Nirvanapada', although it may not have had exclusively Buddhist connotations at the time.

His successor, Udayadityavarman II (1050-1066) constructed the colossal temple-mountain of Bapuon, of which the *gopuras* (elaborate entrances or pavilions) of the second enclosure are decorated with marvellous narrative panels. Their style is very similar to those from Prasat San Kev, built to the south-east of Koh Ker. To him is also attributed the construction of the West Mebon temple and the placing of a large bronze statue of Vishnu in the middle of the *baray*.

Several no less important kings followed, until the accession to the throne of Suryavarman II (c.1100-c.1150) at the age of 16. He became a warrior king, and one of the most important Khmer rulers. He built the greatest masterpiece of Khmer art and a symbol of his power, Angkor Wat temple. That he was a Vishnuite, rather than a follower of Shiva, is attested by the predilection in the famous sculptural relief panels of the temple for stories focusing on the myths of Vishnu, Krishna and Rama. During his reign several other important temples were built in the capital: Preah Pithu, Preah Palilay, Chau Say

3 King Suryavarman II.
Angkor Wat, third enclosure gallery, SW wing.

Tevoda, Thommanon, and Banteay Samre; provincial temples included Preah Khan of Kompong Svay, Beng Mealea, and Phimai (northeast Thailand, initiated by Jayavarman VI, a Buddhist king).

Following the death of Suryavarman II, there was a return to disorder and a weakening of the king's authority. The fierce 1177 raid of the Chams, who pillaged and burned the wooden city to the ground, left the Khmers totally devastated. This was one of the many wars that the Khmers had to sustain against the Chams (from Vietnam) and later the Siamese (today's Thai); therefore, it is not surprising that battle scenes often figure in the reliefs.

In 1181, however, a king from a new dynasty regained control, the mighty Jayavarman VII (1181-1219). He had the capital reconstructed (around the year 1200) in the same place as before, and also rebuilt the royal city, Angkor Thom, centred around the Bayon temple, surrounded by 11 km of massive walls with five monumental gates. The king was a devotee of Mahayana Buddhism, and may have adopted the Tantric concept of the *mandala* (magic circle) as a base for the plan of Bayon. More building projects were begun during his rule than in all previous times. To mention a few: the temples of Banteay Chhmar, Ta Prohm, Preah Khan, Banteay Kdei, and Neak Pean, the terraces of the Elephants and of the 'Leper king', Preah Palilay, the Jayatataka *baray*, 102 'hospitals', the function

of which has not yet been established, and a series of rest-houses, small stone temples for the pilgrims to rest and pray.

It is known that Jayavarman VII was a fervent Buddhist and that he did all he could to affirm his faith. He also exercised a great tolerance for Hindu beliefs as evidenced by the sanctuaries of Preah Khan and Bayon. The latter is actually a pantheon consisting of a Buddhist core surrounded by Vishnuite divinities to the West, Shivaite to the North, and shrines to the memory of the old Khmer kings to the South.

During his rule, Jayavarman VII extended the boundaries of the Khmer empire, supported by a formidable infrastructure controlling hydraulic works, roads, bridges, schools and hospitals. The boundaries of the Khmer empire were extended to the borders of Pagan in Burma, Vientiane in Laos, and to part of the Malay peninsula. The date of Jayavarman VII's death is unknown; perhaps 1220, as indicated by the end of Khmer influence in Champa.

His successor-but-one was Jayavarman VIII, who reigned for a long time and re-introduced Shivaism, causing the destruction of all Mahayana images (but sparing the Theravada sanctuary of Preah Palilay); it is also possible that he completed many of the buildings initiated by Jayavarman VII.

In 1283, during his reign, the Mongols carried out raids in Cambodia, which, were not overly destructive. It was in this period, from 1296-97, that the Chinese traveller Zhou Daguan visited Cambodia and wrote his famous records, marvelling at the country's wealth and customs.

Even after Jayavarman VIII's death, Angkor continued to be magnificent for many decades, before entering a period of social and political weakness, which, combined with the increase in power of the neighbouring Thai polity of Ayutthaya, and the expansion of Champa to the east, contributed to the rapid decline and end of Khmer supremacy around the middle of the 15th century.

After the abandonment of Angkor as the Khmer capital around 1431, the 16th century King Ang Chan I (1516-66) and his son

Paramaraja I (1566-1576) reoccupied the area for a short time to make Angkor the capital of the kingdom once again. During this period they had the reliefs of the North-East quadrant of Angkor Wat completed on the basis of the old original design, by artists who were both strongly influenced by the style of Ayutthaya and introduced Chinese elements. Although a Buddhist king, the Vishnuite content of these reliefs was probably determined out of respect for his great predecessors, and to underline the continuity of royal power, and the superiority of divine being over evil forces. This had a parallel with the Buddhist doctrine that Angkor Wat had assumed after its transformation into a major sanctuary.

More likely it was during this period that modifications and transformations of Angkorean buildings into Buddhist sanctuaries took place, as, for example, at Shrine X of Preah Pithu, and the architectural changes at Wat Nokor (Kompong Cham), where the four pediments of the main sanctuary were sculpted with stories of the life of Buddha. During the 16th century, several colossal Buddha statues were built, by re-using temple stones, at Phnom Bakheng, Bapuon, and, in the case of Phnom Kulen, by sculpting directly into the rock.

Date of accession	King
802	Jayavarman II
835	Jayavarman III
877	Indravarman I
889	Yashovarman I
910	Harshavarman I
922	Ishanavarman II
928	Jayavarman IV
942	Harshavarman II
944	Rajendravarman
968	Jayavarman V
1001	Udayadityavarman I
1002	Jayaviravarman
1002	Suryavarman I
1050	Udayadityavarman II
1066	Harshavarman III
1080	Jayavarman VI
1107	Dharanindravarman I
1113	Suryavarman II
1150	Dharanindravarman II
1160	Yashovarman II
1166	Tribhuvanaditya varman
1181	Jayavarman VII
1219	Indravarman II
1243	Jayavarman VIII
1296	Indravarman III
?1299	Shrindravarman
1309	Shrindrajayavarman
1327	Jayavarman-Parameshvara
1327	End of the Angkorean Period
1432	Final conquest by the Siamese

Simplified List of Angkorean Kings

Buildings	Capital
Kulen	Indrapura, Hariharalaya, Amarandrapura, Kulen
Preah Ko, Indratataka (baray), Bakong	Hariharalaya
East Baray (Yashovaratataka), Lolei, Bakheng, Phnom Krom, Phnom Bok P. Kravan, Baksei Chamkrong	Yashodharapura = 1st Angkor
Koh Ker, Wat Phu (Laos)	Koh Ker
East Mebon, Pre Rup, Srah Srang, Banteay Srei B.Srei (completed), Ta Keo (initiated), North Khleang	Yashodharapura
Ta Keo, West Baray (started), Royal palace, Phimeanakas, South Khleang, Preah Vihear, Phnom Chisor Bapuon Phimai (Thailand) Angkor Wat, Beng Mealea, Preah Khan of Kompong Svay, Chau Say Tevoda, Thommanon, Banteay Samre ? Preah Palilay	2nd Angkor
Ta Prohm, Preah Khan, Jayatataka, Neak Pean, Ta Som, Bayon, ?Banteay Kdei, Terraces of Srah Srang, of the Elephants, of the Leper King, Angkor Thom main doors, rest-houses and more than 100 hospitals, Banteay Chhmar ? completion of many of Jayavarman VII's monuments, defacing of Mahayana icons Mangalartha (last Angkorean stone temple)	3rd Angkor, Angkor Thom

LOCAL BELIEFS AND ANIMISM

For the majority of the Khmer population, the old cults of animism and ancestor worship were the religion of everyday life. Their rituals may have been more discreet than those of the official religion, being restricted to the individual or the community. There is no evidence for this assumption, but comparisons with modern Southeast Asia and particularly Cambodia would support the view.

Today's genii and local powerful spirits of nature, the *neak ta*, are well integrated with the official religion. It is also modern practice to combine a form of Theravada Buddhism with the belief in divinities, with the *devata* (divinity) situated higher than the *neak ta* (spirit). The *neak ta* can be defined as the ancestral spirits of the neighbourhood, or the village, associated with the hills, mounds, trees, etc., where they reside. They are very powerful, and each village community had its *neak ta*, an ancestral spirit, or a number of them, constrained by ritual to the protection of the place. They thus become patron spirits of the community, similar to the *nats* of Burma.

Little is known of these local divinities, perhaps because all inscriptions dealing with religious matters were addressed to Hindu Gods and were in Sanskrit, the gods' own language, unknown to the population at large.

THE CULT OF ANCESTORS

This widespread cult came to Cambodia with the diffusion of Indian traditions.

In early times, it was practised by the families of Brahmins, important soldiers and civil servants, in temples that could be called 'ancestor temples'. The Brahmins played a very important role at the courts of the kings, even more than in India, being their spiritual teachers and counsellors, overseeing the great religious ceremonials essential to the well being of the state. Therefore it was normal, too, for them to have ancestor temples; of these, Banteay Srei is the best example.

The basic concept of this ancestor worship is that if a dignitary had obtained a favour from the

4 Dancing Shiva, Banteay Srei.

king, he would try to continue the benefit for his heirs by building, or restoring, a shrine or temple to a divinity of his liking, possibly related to that of his ancestors. The founder would thus perform a pious act bringing him merits that would be transferred to his relatives; the latter, in return, would assist the founder, and ask the divinities to remain in the shrine forever.

RELIGION

Having adopted the basic principles of Indian religions, particularly the cult of Shiva, the Khmers did not significantly change them, perhaps because they were never totally assimilated. Similarly, Buddhism, accepted mainly in the Mahayana form during the Angkorean period, did not split into sects.

Hinduism The divinities of the Hindu Trinity, Brahma, Shiva and Vishnu, inspired religious cults that became important forms of worship at Angkor. Shivaism was the earliest and most important. However it was temporarily supplanted by Vishnuism in the eleventh century.

Shivaism was certainly practised in Cambodia from the 5th century and remained very popular because it absorbed local beliefs, becoming thus a religion for the people (Bhattacharya, 1961). Shiva was worshipped under the name of Bhadeshvara and the king had to pay him tribute in special ceremonies during which he ascended the sacred mountain at night for a rite involving human sacrifices (according to Zhou Daguan, who admitted he was quoting rumours related by the Chinese residents of Angkor).

The epigraphy indicates the presence of two sects, that of Pasupata (from the 7th century) and that of Shaiva (from the 9th century). The followers of Shiva did not promote caste subdivisions but requested devotion (*bhakti*) towards their god, and it seems that the generic term 'brahmin' was applicable to all followers. Shivaism emphasised Yoga practices; it is curious that Zhou Daguan confused the attitudes and thinking of the ascetics of Shiva with those of Taoist masters!

In Pre-Angkorean times, Shiva was represented mainly in the form of a *linga*. Anthropomorphic representations, however, rare in Pre-Angkorean sculpture, become frequent during the Angkorean period. One of the favourite forms is that of Shiva (*Mahesvara*) with his consort Uma (also known as Parvati, Devi, and Durga in her fierce form) sitting on his left leg (**56,** page 49), sometimes with both mounted on the bull Nandi. Frequently Shiva holds his attribute of the trident or the rosary of the ascetics, in conformity with Indian traditions. His 'in meditation' form at Preah Pithu, or dancing form (*Natakeshvara*) (**127**, page 91) also played an important part in Angkorean iconography. The cult of *Ardhanarishvara*, or androgynous Shiva was rare. The Khmers regarded Shiva as a benevolent

deity, another creator, rather than the fierce and cruel destroyer of Indian mythology.

The consort of Shiva was highly venerated by the Khmers. Often represented with four arms and with a typical hairdo (*kirita-mukuta*) as *Mahisasura-mardini*, she appears in reliefs at Banteay Samre, fighting a demon buffalo standing on a lion, and at Banteay Srei (**125**, page 90) where she has eight arms.

The Linga One of the main attributes of Shiva, the god of fertility, was the phallic symbol of the *linga*. With the elevation of Jayavarman II to *devaraja*, the *linga* cult became a religious, rather than simply a personal cult, as it had been with previous kings. From now on, the prosperity of the kingdom was considered to be bound up with the welfare of the royal *linga*.

The original miraculous *linga* was supposed to have been obtained from Shiva through a Brahmin who gave it to the first king of the dynasty in a ceremony on the sacred mountain at

5 Lingas *in the garden of the Angkor Conservancy, Siem Reap.*

the centre of the city. The king participated with Shiva in sovereign attributes of cosmological proportions, and the people's obedience to the king was a gesture of homage that implied the religious rapport known as *bhakti*, the concept of devotion so dominant in Hindu religion. This devotion acknowledged the king's reputation for spiritual achievement becoming thus a uniting element between various regions of the kingdom.

Vishnuism The cult of Vishnu is known in Cambodia in the form of the Pancaratra sect (Bhattacharya, 1961), as attested by inscriptions. By the end of the 10th century all Vishnuites were designated by the names of Vaishnava, Pancaratra, Bhagavata or Satvata, and King Yashovarman I (889-900) dedicated to them an *ashrama* at Prasat Komnap. The Pancaratra doctrine adopted daily rites five times a day, the concept of five elements and of the four incarnations (*vyuha*) of Vishnu, of which the qualities are supernatural and not natural as

required by the orthodox doctrine. Vishnu is identified with the absolute Brahmin *Purusottama* (Supreme being), and from him emanated the Trinity. He is the cause of the creation, maintenance and dissolution of the Universe; he is unique, transcendent and immanent. He is represented, in general, with four arms holding the attributes of the disc, the conch, the mace and the bowl. Exceptionally, as at Phnom Da, he is represented with eight arms.

Of the *avatar* of Vishnu, *Anantasayin* (on the *naga* Ananta) has enjoyed a particular place in Khmer mythology, as attested by the inscriptions of Bakheng and Prasat Trapeang Run (11th century). Sculptures are known from the 7th century, of Vishnu lying on Ananta on the ocean, respectively symbolising the original chaos and the primordial waters (*42*, page 43). The ocean is also associated with Vishnu in the famous myth of the Churning of the Ocean of Milk, portrayed at Angkor Wat. The most popular representation of the god, however, is when he is mounted on *Garuda*, the half-man, half-bird figure, (*Garudavadhana*), as portrayed in most temples.

Vishnu *Trivikrama* was venerated in Cambodia in the 10th century, with reference to the three steps with which the god created the world, as seen in the reliefs of Prasat Kravan, Bapuon, Banteay Samre, and Preah Pithu. However, in this incarnation, the god's image differs substantially from the those portrayed in India. Another *avatar*, Krishna *Govardhanadhara*, in which Krishna lifts Mount Govardhana, was common during Pre-Angkorean times. During the Angkorean period, however, the popularity of Vishnu increased remarkably with the illustration of the *Ramayana* stories, where he appears in the incarnation of Rama.

The *avatar* of the turtle played a great role in Khmer iconography since it was associated with the Churning of the Ocean of Milk, and Khmer artists reproduced it on many occasions, in particular at the entrance of Vishnu sanctuaries.

Finally, the consort of Vishnu, Lakshmi is often shown with him in sculpture and reliefs; these sometimes being confused with Shiva and his consort Uma.

6 Vishnu on Garuda. Prasat Kravan. (Photo: M. Freeman)

7 Vishnu as the turtle, Kurma, from the Churning of the Ocean of Milk. Angkor Wat. (Photo: M. Freeman)

Other Hindu Cults It seems that in Cambodia Brahma and his spouse Sarasvati were adored together with other members of the Hindu trinity, but there are no proofs of a cult of Brahma himself (Bhattacharya, 1961).

Surya, the Lord Sun, is considered to represent Shiva, as well as Agni, God of Fire, seen as a symbol of the cosmic light of Shiva.

Ganesha enjoyed a certain popularity in Cambodia, although there were no sects dedicated entirely to his cult. In Khmer art he is portrayed with a human body, and not with elephantine limbs as in Javanese art. In Pre-Angkorean times he was known under the name of Ganapati, and was represented, according to the Indian tradition, in the process of eating with his trunk the *modaka* (sweetmeats) placed in one of his hands. In the Angkorean period he took several names (Ganesha, Vighnapati, Vighnesvara, Vighnesa, etc.) and is represented with his broken-off tusk in one of his hands. In general, his features became progressively more human.

Although Khmer syncretism assigned to Shiva and Vishnu a similar position, Shiva was regarded as pre-eminent and Vishnu, without having to admit his inferior rank, was defined as the Absolute. Both the gods are usually invoked in the inscriptions. In order to get the two gods closer, a new divinity was introduced, Harihara, of which the right side is constituted by Shiva and the left half by Vishnu. The cult was popular in Pre-Angkorean times, but faded in the Angkorean period. Syncretism also affected Hinduism and Buddhism.

Certain features which are unknown in Indian mythology must have originated in local beliefs. The Vishnu of Prasat Kravan with a crocodile (or lizard), the *Nataraja* of Banteay Samre with two *asuras* (demons) holding his legs, the *Trivikrama* of the temple of Mangalartha, riding a quadruped, all seem to be deeply rooted in local folklore. Even more characteristic of this tendency is the transformation of the *naga* Ananta into a dragon, and the presence of a rhinoceros as the *vahana* (customary vehicle) of Agni. It is evident that local traditions persisted throughout the period and were progressively incorporated into Hinduism.

Buddhism Although Mahayana Buddhism had some followers in early Angkorean times, it reached its greatest popularity in the late 12th and 13th centuries under the rule of Jayavarman VII (1181 – c.1219). It coexisted with Hinduism in

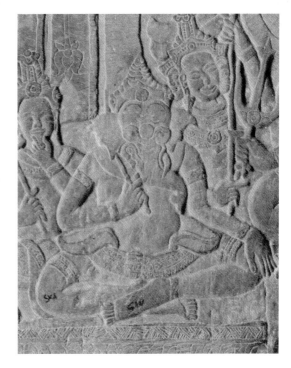

8 Ganesha, from the battle of Krishna against the asura *Bana. Angkor Wat.*

a general form of syncretism, while Theravada Buddhism dominated the post-Angkorean period.

Buddhism was introduced in Cambodia around the same time as Hinduism and coexisted with it in a tolerant way throughout most of the Khmer period. Initially Mahayana Buddhism, the Great Vehicle, was popular, focused on the Buddha Sakyamuni flanked by Bodhisattvas who listened to all supplicants, and had compassion for all human misfortunes, as attested by many sculptures in pre-Angkorean times. It persisted, in a low key, throughout the Angkorean period when Hinduism was the State religion, perhaps with better fortunes during the reign of Suryavarman I.

With the succession of Jayavarman VII, it flourished again and became the state religion, reaching the zenith of its popularity at the end of the 12th and beginning of the 13th century. It emphasised the Buddha as the symbol of victory over suffering, with the Bodhisattva Lokeshvara, the Lord of the Worlds, embodying the divine form of the king, as Shiva and Vishnu had been during previous reigns.

For Jayavarman VII, Buddhism consisted of the worship of a triad consisting of Lokeshvara, the Buddha, and Prajñaparamita, together with the Tantric divinity Hevajra. Although they do not appear in sculptural reliefs, they are symbolically represented in three majestic monuments built by the king: Preah Khan (dedicated to Lokeshvara, 1191), Bayon (with the *naga*-protected Buddha as its principal image), and Ta Prohm (dedicated to Prajñaparamita, 1186).

Tantric or Esoteric Buddhism became increasingly important during the reign of Jayavarman VII; Hevajra, one of the Tantric tutelary deities, was elevated to a new and powerful position. The reason for the shift to this form of Buddhism may have resulted after the catastrophic invasion of the Chams in 1177 showed that the earlier system of religious protection had somehow proved inadequate and a new and more potent theology was required. With the death of Jayavarman VII, the new ruler

9 Bodhisattva Lokeshvara, Neak Pean. (Photo: M. Freeman)

reintroduced Shivaism in an episode of intolerance unique in the history of Southeast Asia, when all Buddhist images in the temples were destroyed. However, about one century later, Theravada (or Hinayana) Buddhism, the Doctrine of the Elders, became the main accepted form of worship. Following the Sinhalese traditions, it conformed strictly to the teaching of the Buddha and his Three Jewels: The Buddha, the Community, and the Law.

With the adoption of Buddhism, arose the need to assemble the faithful and the monks and to give them protection in large buildings. However, these were not large stone edifices, but halls of bricks and wood, sufficient for the faithful to pray and to venerate the sacred images of the Buddha on the altar. In addition, certain

Hindu temples may have been adapted. Certainly, Angkor Wat had, by the 16-17th century, become a Buddhist monastery.

Devaraja cult This cult was initiated by Jayavarman II, in 802, when he was crowned *chakravartin* ('universal sovereign', 'king of kings', king of the Khmer world), some 10 years after he, as an ordinary king, had managed to subdue other Khmer kings. He then appointed a Brahmin to elevate a local god of the deities to a similar rank, as king of the local deities, the supreme protectors of Khmer land (Jacques, 1997). This king of the gods corresponded with the Khmer expression of *kamrateng jagat ta raja*, which translated in Sanskrit is the *devaraja* ('the god who is king'), the king of gods, who was to be incarnated as a miraculous *linga*. The *devaraja* was, in a way, a double of the human sovereign. Erroneously, it has been interpreted as a 'god-king', a god with the essence of the king himself.

Jayavarman II also put a priest in charge of this divinity and decided that his appointment was going to be hereditary. The *devaraja* became the religious symbol of the royal power, thus initiating a national cult. Little is actually known about the *devaraja*, being mentioned only once, in an inscription of the 11th century, and it is possible that Western scholars have over-emphasised its importance.

Religious Syncretism As mentioned above, the Khmers had a relaxed attitude towards religious beliefs, adopting an eclectic approach. The main uniting factor was the cult of the royal *linga* through the *devaraja*, a symbol of power, divine authority and unity. The final amalgamation of this concept of syncretism with Buddhism happened during the reign of Jayavarman VII when he installed the *buddharaja* (a statue of Buddha), instead of the royal *linga*, in the central shrine of Bayon.

KHMER ART AND ARCHITECTURE
14 periods have been established by French scholars for Khmer art and architecture, on the basis, firstly of epigraphic evidence (inscriptions on stele), and secondly on the evolution of aesthetic and architectural elements (temple architecture, decorative elements, the style of the reliefs, etc.). The latter are obviously related to the historic and aesthetic tastes in vogue at the time when the French scholars made their important studies.

Only buildings in brick and stone have been preserved, all others in perishable material having been lost. Archaeological and historical evidence has confirmed that there was a civil, military and religious urbanism, with extensive hydraulic works consisting of the *barays* and thousands of canals and dams, bridges and roads. But the most striking feature of Khmer civilisation is its temples.

The temple was conceived according to the Indian tradition of a temple-mountain, recreating on earth the mountain abode of the gods, Mount Meru, located north of the Himalayas, and traditionally surrounded by water (seas, rivers, lakes) symbolically represented by the moats built around the temple, and the adjacent *barays*. The building followed rigorous rules of measurements and perhaps astronomical alignments.

Initially, from Pre-Angkorean times until the 10th century, the temple was built at the top of natural high ground, a hill, to represent a temple-mountain, with a simple square plan for one shrine in which to preserve and protect the sacred *linga*. The temple was surrounded by a ditch with a raised access along the axis of the shrine's main entrance door, which was adorned with carved lintels.

Gradually, the temple was modified to assume the shape of a step-pyramid. During the 11th century, the temple-mountain was further developed with the addition of a sequence of monumental terraces. The various elements became progressively more complex, with enclosure walls all around, elaborate *gopuras*, and more buildings as annexes to the shrine, such as

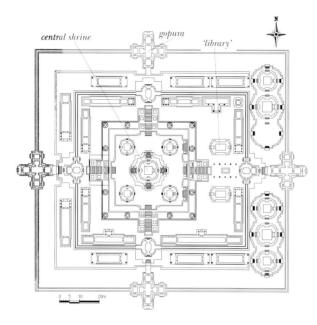

central shrine   gopura   'library'   N

10 *The concentric plan of Pre Rup.*

the so-called 'libraries', whose real function remains unclear. Some temples grouped together several sanctuaries, usually in odd numbers.

The plan of the temple evolved from square to cruciform to central-circular. During the Angkorean period there were two major types of plan for the temples: the centred plan with buildings grouped within concentric enclosure walls (*10*), and the axial plan with the main and subsidiary buildings arranged along a linear axis such as at Koh Ker.

Despite the marvels of Angkor Wat and Bayon, a great deal of Khmer architecture was poorly executed, either using inferior materials (wood, laterite, sandstone which was often soft) or using them in an unsafe way.

Technically, the Khmers did not go beyond the stage of the simple vault (arch) created by superimposing slabs, in a technique called corbelling, limited by the burden of the weight. As a consequence, they could not build large rooms inside the temple shrines, but only narrow cells and connecting galleries. The impressive transformation in the art of Khmer temple building, from the simple single cell of pre-

Angkorean times to the complexity of Angkor Wat, corresponds to an expansion in social organisation, the structuring of labour and organisation of construction work, and the development of irrigated agriculture and seasonal cropping to produce a food surplus.

Architectural Symbolism No treatises dealing with the Khmer laws of architecture have been found, but it is likely that Khmer architects and builders may have had some knowledge of the basic books of Indian architecture (*shastra*), like the *Manasura* and the *Mayamata*.

Scholars such as René Dumont, Pierre Grison and Philippe Paris have proposed theories which, besides clarifying the essential laws of architecture, should also lead to an understanding of the astronomical and cosmological symbolism of the temples. More recently, Eleanor Mannikka has published the results of her 20 years of research on Angkor Wat, focusing on its measurements. Their studies have looked at the following aspects which may have formed the basis of Khmer architecture:

a) accurate geographic measurements of the distances existing between the temples, which may establish a meaningful network pattern between the sites.

b) a detailed study of the alignments within the architectural elements of a temple in relation to the trajectory of the sun, and the importance of the ritual alignment along the cardinal points, leading to an astronomical and cosmic symbolism.

c) accurate measurements of the geometric patterns and their organisation within the plan of the temple, which may reflect different underlying symbolic *mandala*.

d) an assessment of the numbers which seem to have been used in multiples of a basic unit of measurement, known from Indian numerology, arranged in patterns throughout the temple, reflecting a cosmic symbolism.

Stone proof of the symbolism of Khmer architecture may be seen in a stele at the south-eastern corner of Bayon's wall. In it, the city of Angkor Thom is compared to Sudharma, the

11 Guardian at the east entrance of Angkor Thom.
(Photo: M. Freeman)

assembly-hall of the gods at the summit of Mount
Meru. Although they were Mahayanists, the
builders drew their inspiration from Sanskrit
sources, in order to create (at the five gates of the
city) the five guardians of the 33 gods, the *yakshas*
pulling the *nagas* on the bridges in front of the
gates, the four great kings looking over the four
cardinal points (the famous face towers on the
gates), and the images of Indra, sculpted at the
corners of the gates, mounted on the three-
headed elephant Airavata.

   This symbolism tallies with the great interest
of the Khmers in the stories of the battles
between the *devas* (gods) and the *asuras* (devilish
monsters), always aiming to destroy the city of the
gods. Moreover, since the Khmer kingdom
represented the world of the gods (Phimeanakas
inscription), and the Chams the *asuras*, the

offensive of the latter against the Khmers had to
end in disaster for the assailants, just as the
asuras' attack on the divine city of Indra ended,
after a short-lived victory due to the advantage of
surprise. Thus the effective system of defence
provided by Jayavarman VII was said to be
identical to the one installed by Indra for the
divine city in order to prevent any new offensive
by the *asuras* (Boisselier, 1993).

FUNCTION OF RELIEFS

Western scholars have argued endlessly about the
scope and *raison d'etre* of the reliefs, as well as the
possibility of whether their meaning is closely
related to their function. Modern views tend to
interpret the reliefs sculpted in the temples as a
sort of encoded text containing important
Angkorean religious, mythological, historical,
ethic and moral concepts. This weakens earlier
interpretations that they were purely ornamental
and decorative elements enhancing the aesthetic
value of the architecture, and favours the view
that their function stemmed from important
concepts held by their builders.

   There is no evidence that there was a
programme which reserved relief carving for a
particular part of the galleries of the temple.
However, on the basis of the close relationship of
the king with his god, the exclusivity of the
Brahmin caste, and the adoption of secret and
magic rites and rituals, it is reasonable to assume
that the reliefs, particularly within the first and
second enclosures, were not accessible to the
public.

   The stories narrated in the reliefs may have
been addressed only to members of the royal
family and of the religious establishment, rather
than aiming to educate and illuminate the
pilgrims or the visitors to the temple. It is
possible, however, that people were allowed to see
reliefs in some parts of the temples during
celebrations of special importance, but even then,
accompanied by religious instructors. Many
reliefs, particularly the ones from Angkor Wat
and Bayon, must have been difficult to 'read' by
the uninitiated.

It is evident that the Khmers followed Indian texts, whose iconography clearly influenced the image-making process. The version of the texts and the style of their Sanskrit sentences, more or less elaborate and detailed, would also affect the creation of the images. It is very possible, therefore, that the Khmer reliefs were mediated by the priests, and not 'read' directly by the layman. They appealed to the already established knowledge of the elite who could easily recognise the scenes depicted. In all likelihood, the Brahmins had been involved in the original conception of the content of the reliefs.

Magic function Cœdès (1936) was of the opinion that in Khmer sculpture, the role of the decoration (reliefs and statues) of the monuments was not aesthetic, but had an 'evocative' function, that of animating the temple, of bringing it to life. Reliefs were not made to edify visitors, but to contribute to the realisation and materialisation on earth of the divine world.

Thus the reliefs of Angkor Wat narrating the stories of King Suryavarman II, and those of Bayon dealing with King Jayavarman VII, gave life to the temples by making the presence of these kings become real. With this in mind, it was essential for the images to be exact, correct in every detail, otherwise they would fail in their objective, just as in a magic ceremony where the essential rite was omitted or wrongly performed. This resulted in the sculptors following in great detail specific texts or a particular iconographic tradition that they could master well enough to make their interpretation unambiguous. If not, the identification of the scenes would be doubtful or incomplete, if not impossible.

Later, Cœdès (1943 and 1964) developed his theory of the magic function of the reliefs in transforming the temple into a celestial building, by pointing out that the celestial palaces from the reliefs of Heavens and Hells at Angkor Wat are in the shape of flying pavilions supported by *garudas* and lions. Similarly, the presence of *garudas*/caryatids at the Royal Terrace also transformed it symbolically into a flying palace.

The importance of the 'flying palaces' in Khmer mythology goes back to an ancient local legend (Marchal, 1955).There was a young prince by the name of Prea Ket Mealea, son of the king of Indraprastha (old name of Cambodia), who was both beautiful and perfect. His qualities were so outstanding that the god Indra living on Mount Meru in the sky, came to earth to abduct him. After a while, the *devatas* (celestial beings like the *apsaras* but living on Mount Meru), complained about his human smell and expressed their dissatisfaction with Indra. The latter felt obliged to please the *devatas* and had the prince sent back to earth. However, to comfort him, he had a palace, exactly like the one in the sky that the prince appreciated so much, built by all the celestial people, including the architect of the gods, Prea Pusnuka; the location was decided by the bull Nandi to the east-south-east of Phnom Bakheng.

Most of the Pre-Angkorean temples of Sambor Prei Kuk (600-650) are decorated with reliefs of representations of small ornate architectural dwellings, with or without people, supported by winged personages and animals, representing just such *vimana* or flying palaces in which the gods and deities move through space.

Since they do not reproduce known Indian buildings, nor the Khmer buildings on which they are sculpted, they clearly display the imagination of the designers or sculptors, giving concrete form to their concept of celestial flying palaces.

Religious function According to Glaize (1944), Khmer temples were not places of public worship (as in the West), but personal monuments that kings or aristocrats had piously erected with the aim of obtaining 'merit' which would be transmitted to all the participants. Only on special occasions were the reliefs accessible to the believers and pilgrims who would walk in procession to see and, possibly, read them. This opinion was based on previous studies by Cœdès, who, on the basis of epigraphic discoveries at that time, thought that the main royal temples were funerary temples, mausoleums and tombs, with the ashes of the deceased being dispersed on the statues representing the deceased under divine form. They were not public temples or places of pilgrimage, but the last dwelling, like a palace, wherein Khmer kings returned to their divine aspect. The discovery of stone containers, similar to sarcophagi, reinforced the conclusion that Angkorean monuments were both temples and mausoleums, where a statue representing the subject with god-like traits was erected, assimilating him to a god.

Decorative function Coral de Remusat (1951) believed that the narrative reliefs had a purely decorative function, like those with ornamental motifs taken from the animal and vegetal kingdoms and from jewellery. Therefore, the narrative reliefs had meanings of their own, and could be considered in isolation, without taking into account the architectural elements to which they belonged.

Reading order This topic, discussed mainly with reference to the Angkor Wat reliefs, has stimulated much debate. Le Bonheur (1989) has rightly commented that nothing proves that the reliefs have to be read in sequence, one after the other, nor in an unique pre-determined order. The existence of chambers with doors along the galleries and corner pavilions would make any progressive 'reading' very arduous.

Also, the circumambulation order is totally unproven, including the idea that it was to be done by keeping the temple to the left, if in the funerary way *(prasaya)*, or to the right if in the ceremonial way *(pradakshina)*, presumably while reading all the reliefs, one after the other.

Even if one attributes a funerary function to Angkor Wat (also unproven), it does not follow that the processions which may have taken place in the *prasaya* direction, had as their objective the reading of the reliefs! Processions would also have been physically difficult, as the corridors were narrow and often broken by the high steps of the cells or shrines.

Le Bonheur (1995) is of the opinion that it would be vain to seek a sequential order for the eight large reliefs of Angkor Wat. Rather their location would seem to reflect the importance paid to the symbolism of the cardinal points. The exceptional opening of the temple to the West meant that, at Angkor Wat, West was the most important cardinal direction, followed, according to the rules, by the South, again in contrast to all other Khmer temples, where the hierarchical order would privilege the North. Therefore the SW quadrant was probably privileged in relation to the NE quadrant, and this is proved by the fact that in the latter the reliefs were completed only in the 16th century.

According to Jacques (1990), the Bapuon reliefs, arranged in superimposed panels, are to be read from bottom to top. If one knows the plot of the story, the sequence of events narrated should give a clear enough indication of the direction of reading.

An episode which sheds light, if not on the reading order, but on how the sculptors worked, concerns the reliefs at Phnom Rung. Here, according to Pichard (1974), the areas lower down were carved first simply because the sculptors had to wait for the scaffolding to be built by the carpenters. Once the scaffolding was set up, the work could proceed from the top down.

12 Detail of Soldiers. Angkor Wat, S gallery, W wing.

THE NARRATIVE OF THE SCULPTURAL RELIEFS

This book focuses on Khmer reliefs, mainly executed in stone, dating from the 9th to the 13th centuries. In particular, it concentrates on the narrative of the reliefs, and it is appropriate here to clarify the meaning of these terms.

By 'narrative' is meant a series of logically and chronologically related events caused, or experienced, by the protagonist/s (personage/s), which is presented, or organised, in a certain manner, or order.

In other words, narrative means the narrating of relevant facts, recounting a story, a legend or a scene, as a single episode (event) or a series of episodes (events) over time.

The narrative technique of Khmer reliefs – like any other – includes two main elements: the material that is worked into the story, i.e. events, actors, location and time, and a certain way of presenting this material. The events are transitions from one state to another, and the actors the agents performing actions (kings, gods, soldiers, Khmer people, elephants, and so on).

The various elements are put together in a specific story. The order of presentation and the point of view from which the elements are presented (perspective), has a great influence on the narrative. The arrangement of the events, the patterning of the story as relief sculpture, can be rendered in a sequence, panel by panel.

In Khmer reliefs, the events narrated refer to selected events from Indian or Buddhist mythology (*Mahabharata*, *Ramayana*, Buddha stories), or to facts of Khmer history (Royal procession, Naval Battle against the Chams). There is also another class of relief, famous from the Bayon, showing scenes from daily life which are not truly part of a 'narrative', not strictly speaking part Khmer mythology.

By 'relief' is meant the carving of stone, usually shallow, commonly referred to as low-reliefs or bas-reliefs.

In general, the medium used allows only the representation of a particular moment in time. Therefore, the representation involves either specific moments of a particular event, or various episodes in one or more events. Sometimes the stories are represented in a single panel such as 'The Battle of Kurukshetra' (Angkor Wat), or in panels divided into superimposed registers, such as the 'Heavens and Hells' reliefs (Angkor Wat) or in almost all the Bayon reliefs. A third type shows a series of panels in a continuos narrative such as at Bapuon.

The term 'sculptor' is used in a generalised sense, acknowledging that the reliefs have been conceived, designed and drawn probably by many people, and not necessarily the sculptor, before being actually carved in low relief on stone. Indeed, 'image makers' may be a more appropriate term. In India, material images to be produced for worship must be executed by a professional craftsman, who may be designated with different names such as *silpin* = craftsman, yogin = *yogi*, *sadhaka* = adept, or simply *rupakara*, or *pratimakara* = imager (Coomaraswamy, 1956).

WOMEN IN KHMER ART AND SOCIETY

In Khmer mythology and society, man is the very centre of the world; women define themselves almost exclusively in relation to this all-powerful other. Society's main concern was the distinction between the status of formal wives and that of concubines, who in both categories could be numerous. For the king, the most important figure was that of the main wife, the *agramahishi* who, in her position of royal consort and mother of the king's progeny, would assume considerable influence in Khmer society.

She had a commanding role in the royal palace and, if she gave the kings sons, one of whom was destined to become king, she would rise to a higher rank. She could even appoint the new heir to the throne, in a climate full of conspiracies, assassinations and usurpers.

In the absence of a direct heir to the throne, a member of the royal family could become eligible through the lineage of his mother or wife. Equally, when a king was too young to rule, the regent was often chosen through the female lineage. Usurpers married the daughter or widow of their predecessors in an attempt to legitimise their royal status. Therefore, it is evident that, at least at the royal level, for the Khmers the matriarchal system was as important as the patriarchal one, if not more so.

Little is known about the role of ordinary women in Khmer history. The only well-documented female figures are the wives of Jayavarman VII. His main wife was Indradevi to whom he gave the title of principal queen (*agramahishi*), after the death of his first wife, Jayarajadevi, eldest sister of Indradevi.

The great stele of Phimeanakas, composed by Indradevi in memory of her sister, reveals the character of those two princesses. Jayarajadevi married Jayavarman when he was still a prince, and followed his fortune, often involving long separations from him, worrying about his fate. She spent almost all her life in strict penance in order to obtain the success and return of her husband. Despite all this hardship, her beauty was not affected. In her spiritual exercises she was instructed by her sister Indradevi, to consider the Buddha as the beloved who could be reached through the fire of torments and the sea of pain.

When Jayavarman VII returned triumphant to Angkor as king of kings, she was so thankful that she decided, together with her husband, to disperse on earth all their wealth, by making it available to the gods and the poor, through the donation of ritual objects worthy of the royal treasure, and by nourishing those in need. Unfortunately, her happiness was short-lived and, perhaps consumed by too many strict ascetic practices, and, according to an inscription, "despite her eternal loyalty to the beloved husband, soon after her master was invested of more power, she entered the *nirvana*". Her death filled the king with sorrow, and he crowned her younger sister Indradevi as queen, placating the "fire of pain that was burning the world".

Indradevi was said to be a woman full of grace, pure and devoted to her king, and a person of great culture and intelligence. She was appointed by the king as the main teacher of two important temples where she was "always distributing her knowledge to a crowd of women" (Phimeanakas stele).

This is not the place for a critical essay on the role of female protagonists of the great Indian epics; however, it seems that, in general, women were treated as passive elements in the narrative. They existed to respond to the passion of the males, but not initiate it. It is not surprising, therefore, that in Khmer iconography too, women do not play a significant role. Their celestial counterparts, the *apsaras*, were very popular, however, and appeared in most of the narrative reliefs in association with the gods, watching and supporting their actions. Less common were the

13 *Market women. Bayon, Outer gallery. (Photo: M. Freeman)*

14 *King Jayavarman VII. Bayon, Inner gallery. (Photo: EFEO)*

devatas, pure female beings of the gods' paradise, who amongst their other roles, had the function of guarding the main doors of the temples.

An example of earthly women's involvement in the royal household can be found in Zhou Daguan's description, in the 13th century, of a troop of "girls holding shields and lances (spears), the bodyguard of the palace" accompanying the king whenever he left the palace. Perhaps a 'precedent' for this occurs in a pediment at Angkor Wat interpreted as showing a *naga* princess fighting Prince Kaundinya, with an army of women (***189***, page 125), unique in Khmer art (Bhandari, 1995).

In addition, Henri Mouhot, in the account of his *Travels in Siam, Cambodia and Laos, 1858-1860*, illustrates a picturesque 'Amazon of the king's female guard' which was in place at the time of his visit.

16 Apsara. *(Photo: M. Freeman)*

15 *Princess in a boat. Bayon, Inner gallery. (Photo: M. Freeman)*

Simplified Chronology of Khmer Styles

Period		Year	Style
Pre-Angkorean	Funan	300-450	'Funan'
		540-450	Phnom Da
	Chenla	600-650	Prei Kuk
		700-750	Prasat Andet
		706-825	Kompong Preah
Transition		825-875	Phnom Kulen
Angkorean	Early	875-893	Preah Ko
		893-925	Bakeng
		921-945	Koh Ker
		947-965	Pre Rup
	Middle	946-1000	Banteay Srei
		965-1010	Khleang
		1010-1080	Bapuon
	Late	1100-1175	Angkor Wat
		1177-1230	Bayon
		1230-1431	Post-Bayon
Post-Angkorean		1431 Final conquest of Angkor by Siamese	Lopburi Thai-Khmer

17 *Overleaf: The abduction of Sita by the* rakshasa *Ravana. (Photo: M.Freeman)*

Khmer Myths and Legends

THE SOURCES

The prime sources for Khmer mythology are to be found in the classic Indian Hindu and Buddhist texts.

The great Indian epic poems (written between 400 BC and 400 AD) were based on the concept that history is divided into four cycles or ages (*kalpa*). At the beginning (in the first age), righteousness and order governed the world; however, through the ages, things deteriorated to the point that the gods decided to destroy the world and start a new one. The *Ramayana* is placed within the second age, when order started to come under attack. The *Mahabharata* is set towards the end of the third age, and the civil war narrated therein marks the beginning of the fourth age, the era of final disintegration and injustice. The epics emphasise the need to discover meaning and purpose, even in periods of disorder.

The *Mahabharata* is the chief mythological epic, based on old traditions, perhaps antedating 400 BC, but completed around 300 AD. It is a colossal work full of mythical, ritual, moral and genealogical lore, relating the supernatural origin of the author himself, followed by that of the lineage of the first Indian kings. In time, it became an encyclopaedic repository of ancient myths, legends, laws, and ethical precepts.

At the core of the enormous compendium of the *Mahabharata* (ten times as long as the *Iliad* and *Odyssey* together), is the epic war between the Pandavas and their cousins the Kauravas, culminating in the Battle of Kurukshetra.

In Khmer narrative reliefs, scenes from the *Mahabharata* are rare, with most concentrating on the final battle of Kurukshetra, in contrast to the frequent depiction of *Ramayana* events and Krishna stories. Some scholars include in the *Mahabharata* the account of the Churning of the Ocean of Milk, while others consider it part of the *Bhagavad Purana*.

The *Ramayana* was composed between 200 BC and 200 AD. It narrates, in poetic form, the adventure of Vishnu's incarnation on earth as Prince Rama, as well as, in the first and last books, other important myths.

The *Puranas* are perhaps the greatest source of mythological material and documentation of Indian thought. They exist in many sectarian versions, presenting the same myth in different ways. The most popular in Cambodia seem to have been the *Bhagavad Purana* and the *Harivamsa*, both from the first millennium AD.

Buddhist myths and legends are related to the fundamental text of the *Buddhavamsa* describing the lineage of the Buddha, and to the *jatakas* which include 547 stories of the 24 Buddhas who preceded the historical Buddha. The last, called *Vessantara Jataka* because it tells the story of Prince Vessantara, is an exaltation of the act of giving and ultimate renunciation, and was well known in Cambodia. Both texts had been available in written form since the second century BC. The *jatakas*, mainly transmitted orally according to popular tradition, were extremely popular because of their rich visual imagery that could stir the imagination of the believers.

The life of the historical Buddha, Siddharta Gautama, or Sakyamuni, is told in several versions widespread in Southeast Asia, but none appeared in written form until several centuries after the Buddha's death. The better known texts are the *Buddhacarita* and the shorter *Lalitavistara*, which was the one commonly adopted by the Khmers.

In India and Southeast Asia, some cultures have selected particular events from the classic myths and legends, to express their view of reality. For the *Ramayana*, Richman (1991) noticed that, in some countries, people have challenged the main *Ramayana* traditions by selectively dismembering particular stories. Through this process of abridgement, the events gain power and richness, because they express people's ultimate concerns. A fragment of the text, or some decontextualised incident, is taken to represent the essence of the whole. This search for events which appear to be pregnant with specific meaning to a particular culture, in itself generates new, additional meanings.

A similar selection has taken place in Khmer culture, particularly with regard to the *Ramayana*, and the *Mahabharata*. From the *Ramayana's* two distinct parts – the first recounting historical events centred around the court of King Dasharatha, the second to ancient myths, full of marvels and fantasy– the Khmers chose the latter for their reliefs, thereby revealing their love of the imaginary and of mythological stories.

Within this second part, a further selection has been made with the preferred scenes for large sculptural panels being the battles. There may be various reasons for this. The choice may have been dictated by a powerful king who believed that in real life he was emulating the epic battles of the gods, a sort of military apotheosis. Or the Khmer people, always at war, may have found comfort in imagining that similar sufferings had also been experienced by the heroes of their beloved myths, whom they assimilated perhaps to close ancestors. A more prosaic reason is that battle scenes were the most suitable subjects for filling such large wall surfaces as those presented in the galleries of Angkor Wat and Bayon.

Similarly, in the 18th century Thai version of the *Ramayana*, the *Ramakien*, partings and reunions, such essential events of the Hindu *Ramayana*, are not as important as the excitement and the details of war, the technique, and the fabulous weapons. (Ramanujan, 1991).

Likewise, the Khmer preferred the *Bhagavad Gita* story to events from the main body of the *Mahabharata*. The *Bhagavad Gita*, with its 18-day battle of Kurukshetra, gave greater freedom to the imagination, to the spirit, with the sacrifice of Bishma, and the dialogue between Arjuna and Krishna during the melee.

Goldman in his seminal works on Indian epics, has highlighted the prevalence of 'œdipal' themes, a psychoanalytical approach rejected by most Indologists (1978, 1984). The classic triangle of father-mother-son in Greek mythology, is transformed into one between a *guru* or spiritual preceptor-the *guru's* wife-young male personnage. The best examples can be seen in that of Rama and Deasharatha where Rama demonstrates unhesitating obedience to his father, or in the *Mahabharata* where Babhruvahavana is torn between his duty to fight the intruder, his father Arjuna, and filial submissiveness. Similarly at the beginning of the *Bhaghavad Gita*, Arjuna kills Bishma, the 'grandfather of the Kauravas', and is thus guilty of murdering his adoptive father.

The need to disguise the son's aggressive urges towards his father and erotic attachment to the mother, has led to the notion, both in India and the West, that India has no true œdipal myths. However, in Goldman's view, legends of passive and negative type heroes occupy a special place in Hindu India.

Buddhist myths and legends were also submitted to a process of appropriation or abridgement similar to the one seen above for Hindu mythology. Khmer image-makers made a selection of the episodes of the life of Buddha which would emphasise the compassionate aspect of his teachings. Images of the *Bodhisattvas* were also highlighted to represent the essence of the whole of Mahayana thought.

18 *Krishna and Arjuna. Angkor Wat, W gallery, SW wing. (Photo: J. Poncar)*

THE LEGEND OF RAMA

1. *The Ramayana*

The epic poem of the *Ramayana* tells the story of
Prince Rama, one of the earthly incarnations of
Vishnu. Traditionally it has been divided into
seven major books, or *kandas*, telling Rama's
adventures in chronological sequence.

The best known and most popular version is
the one narrated by the poet Valmiki. However,
the version adopted in Cambodia seems to differ
from it in several places (Martini, 1938), and is
also incomplete, with only a few of the events of
the original Indian text. For instance while, in
Valmiki's text, in order to gain the prize of the
beautiful Sita, Rama had to prove himself able to
lift the magic bow, in the Cambodian version, a
more complex archery competition ensues
requiring the contestant to hit a bird behind a
moving wheel. This variant is not due to a
betrayal of the text, but probably to the need to
follow local versions.

Since the 17th century the Rama legend had
become known in Cambodia as *Reamker* (Saveros
Pou, 1980-90), as in the Khmer language the
name of the hero Rama is 'Ream'. It is also
referred to as *Ramakerti*, Rama's glory, and
Ramakien, Rama's story. The Thai version of the
Ramayana, the *Ramakien*, was based on the
application of Buddhist principles to the story of
Rama, a glorification of the virtue of indifference
to the real world, and acceptance of the *dharma*.
Rama's story crosses the boundaries of caste,
religion, cultural settings, and language, similarly
to Buddhist principles.

The story of the *Ramayana* may briefly be
summarized as follows. In the beginning, a badly
behaved giant, the *rakshasa* Ravana (famous for
shaking Mount Kailasa), had become unbearable
to the gods for all his perfidies and treacheries.
They all went to visit Vishnu, who was lying on
the *naga* Ananta, and implored him to go down
to earth to fight Ravana and re-establish order
and peace. The god agreed to be reincarnated as
Rama, and was born in Ayodhya in the palace of
King Dasharatha as his son.

19 *Rama killing Marica. Angkor Wat, SW corner pavilion.*
(Photo: EFEO)

As a young man, he entered the city of King
Janaka, where, in an archery competition, he
managed to obtain the most cherished prize, Sita,
the beautiful daughter of the king. They were
happily married, and later Rama was announced
heir to the throne in the kingdom of Ayodhaya.
However, his father, because of court intrigues,
changed his mind and ordered his son expelled
from the city and exiled to the wilderness.

Rama willingly renounced his claim to the
succession and left for the forest followed by his
wife Sita, who did not want to leave him, and his
brother Lakshmana, whose devotion to the
married couple would be manifested on many
occasions. During their 14 years of wandering,
many adventures happened, including the
mutilation of the *rakshini* Shurpanakha (sister of
Ravana) who insisted on marrying Rama, the
killing of the *rakshini* Tataka (mother of Marica)
and of the *rakshasa* Marica metamorphosed as a
golden deer as a decoy to distract Rama, the
attempt by the *rakshasa* Viradha to abduct Sita,
and the encounter with the monster Kabandha.
The culminating event was the abduction of Sita
by the wicked king Ravana, ruler of the kingdom
of Lanka. Rama's friend, the vulture Jatayus,
attempted to save Sita but was mortally wounded.
Rama, maddened by grief, and wandering around

the forest searching for his beloved, met Sugriva, an exiled monkey prince, and established an alliance with him, in order to regain his wife. However, in return, he had to kill Valin, Sugriva's usurper brother, in order to re-establish the royal power of Sugriva. Rama could also count on the loyal support of the white monkey general Hanuman, and his strong army of monkeys.

Hanuman was then sent on an expedition to find where Sita had been hidden. After several strange adventures, through the help of the vulture Sampati (brother of Jatayus), he managed to locate her, guarded by *rakshini*, in Ravana's palace in Lanka. Meeeting her in an acacia grove, Hanuman gives her Rama's ring as a sign of his commitment to free her. Apparently, Sita had been treated properly by Ravana, who was not taking advantage of the situation. Hanuman rushed back to rejoin Rama, not without having first burnt Ravana's royal palace with his tail set afire.

Ravana tried to defeat and kill Rama and his army of monkeys but was repulsed with great losses. He responded to the advice of his sage brother Vibhisana to return Sita to Rama and end the gruesome conflict, by exiling Vibhisana from Lanka. The latter joined forces with Rama, and advised him on the best way to defeat Ravana.

Rama decided than to attack Lanka to regain his wife. An extremely fierce battle, the Battle of Lanka, took place between the army of Rama's monkey allies, headed by the mighty Hanuman, holder of magical powers, and Sugriva, against the army of the *rakshasas* headed by Ravana. The outcome was uncertain until Rama killed Ravana in single combat. Also Ravana's son Indrajit (known also as Meghanada) was killed after a gruesome fight with Lakshmana who was badly wounded, but was cured by a magic remedy from Sushena (monkey general, father of Tara).

Rama sent for Sita, but refused to take her back because she had lived in Ravana's palace; he insisted that she must prove her innocence of any infidelity by going through the ordeal of fire. Having survived that ordeal, she was accepted by Rama, and the two were finally reunited. After

crowning Vibhisana as Lanka's wise new king, Rama returned triumphantly to Ayodhya, on his famous chariot Pushpaka, and was crowned king.

In Khmer mythology, the story seems to terminate here, all other events occupying a less significant position, almost as if to avoid resolving crucial elements, like the question of the purity of Sita and her treatment by Rama. The answer to the question of how and why the Khmers selected particular events from the *Ramayana* must lie in their view of reality, and their need to convey political views and inculcate religious teachings.

Valmiki presented Rama, the hero of the story, as a renouncer. Rama was not proud of his martial valour and declined to assert his right to succeed to the throne. When finally enthroned, he refused to protect his beloved wife from the gossip of his people. He accepted all kinds of injustice, while remaining in perfect control of his emotions.

The moral message of the story is that of the triumph of good over evil forces, of love over all obstacles, of brotherhood and supporting friendship, as well as of the teacher-pupil relationship, in so far as Rama has much to teach us by his exemplary conduct.

Some scholars are of the opinion (Goldman, 1990) that the fight of Rama and his monkey allies against the savage *rakshasas* of Lanka may reflect some historical reality. The *rakshasas* may be identified with the various Dravidian and tribal people of Southern India and Sri Lanka, hostile to Aryan penetration. The monkeys, on the contrary, may have been local tribes well-disposed towards the high caste Aryans.

In Cambodia, members of the ruling Khmer class may have seen in the *Ramayana* an analogy to their own situation. They may have realised the importance of alliances with local chiefs of a lower level of culture, to fight against unfriendly savage tribal groups, constantly opposing Khmer rule and expansion. Moreover, the Khmer kings, who may have believed themselves to be incarnations of gods, could compare themselves to Rama, the mythical incarnation of a divinity battling against the forces of evil.

The *Ramayana* assumed the moral function of an exemplary tale, and its hero, Rama, that of an example for human behaviour, the perfect man, an ideal towards which ordinary people should strive. In the daily practice of Indians, he was the perfect son who subordinates the goals of his own life to those of his father, who is loyal to his wife, while remaining the compelling hero of a fundamentally tragic epic tale.

Although the *Ramayana* initially did not have a specific theological function, it acquired one because Rama was the earthly manifestation of the god Vishnu. Therefore the text becomes a devotional text, a holy story which could purge one from one's sins.

At the time of Jayavarman VII, the *Ramayana* was seen as an allegory of the king's life. Like Rama, he had been unjustly exiled, and had to fight evil forces (the Chams being equated with the *rakshasas*), before being able to return to Angkor (Ayodhya in the case of Rama) and regain the throne. Sita was the symbol of Cambodia, and making her free was the objective of the king.

THE CHOICE OF THEMES

Although narrative reliefs illustrating various episodes are common, the battle scenes are the most popular subject, particularly for large scale compositions. The emphasis is generally on the dramatic confrontations between Rama and Ravana and their armies. Related accessories like warriors, riders, archers, monkeys and chariots, form a large part of the fill-in repertory.

In the reliefs, little, or nothing, is told of the myths and legends of the first book, the *Bala Kanda* (concerning Rama's father and his infancy), and of the last book, the *Uttara Kanda* (dealing with events after Sita's rescue, including her repudiation). Possibly the Khmers did not consider them to belong to the purest tradition. Indeed, it has been noticed by modern philologists that these books are more likely to have been later additions. Alternatively, at the time, they may not have been known in Cambodia, or, if known, their content was not agreeable to the elite.

The first popular event is the archery competition to obtain the hand of Sita. Nothing is shown of the marriage of Rama and Sita, nor of their private life. Forest scenes introduce the next prominent events: their exile and wanderings, meeting ascetics, the confrontation with the ogress Shurpanakha. The pursuit and killing of the golden deer appears in a few reliefs. The abduction of Sita is rarely represented, neither is that of the vulture Jatayus who bravely attempted to save her. The favourite events are the ones dealing with Sita in exile, distressed in the acacia bush, and of her receiving the visit of Hanuman to whom she gives a ring for Rama, as a sign of her devotion.

No scenes of the preparations for the battle of Lanka are known in the reliefs, while the climax of the battle itself, the melee, is developed with great narrative fervour. More even than the infantry and the dominant figures of the heroes, Rama and Ravana and their generals, the monkeys are depicted with great verve, becoming thus the real protagonists of the event. They fly through the air attacking Ravana's army, crowding around the main characters in the battle, often grabbing the demon warriors by the hair, biting them, pulling them to pieces. Often they even fight each other in playful attitudes, and sometimes they play drums and dance. In a few instances they shown to be capable of staying quiet, and in compassionate attitudes. Nothing is said about Rama's jealousy, fuelled by his discovery of Sita's portrait Ravana, made during her captivity, which triggered, amongst existing doubts about her fidelity, the trial by fire.

Relief representations of Sita's ordeal are very rare, while the horse sacrifice of Rama is missing, as well as any scene related to Rama and Sita's enthronement.

A selection of the most popular stories represented by Khmer sculptors is given below, with reference only to the most significant, complete and well preserved reliefs. Other stories are illustrated in the chapters dealing with specific temples.

Ravana Shaking Mount Kailasa In this Shivaite story, Mount Kailasa is represented as an elegantly decorated step-pyramid, the residence of people and monsters. The giant Ravana, with many heads and arms, king of the *rakshasas* and ruler of Lanka, goes to this mountain, home of Shiva and his wife Uma, but he is forbidden access by a giant monkey guardian. Furious with rage, he raises the base of the mountain and shakes it to attract the attention of Shiva. All creatures living on the mountain are terrorised, and Uma, with a charming gesture, snuggles against Shiva 's chest. But Shiva, with one simple move, pushes the mountain with his toe causing it to collapse on Ravana who is crushed under the rubble. Ravana acknowledges Shiva's power and sings his praise for 1,000 years; as a reward, Shiva sets him free and gives him a sword.

It is interesting to note this representation of Ravana which conflicts with his depiction elsewhere. In the Shivaite passage of the *Uttarakanda*, probably added later to the Ramayana, Ravana ends up by being blessed by Shiva and even receives a magic weapon. In other parts of the *Ramayana*, Ravana is depicted as an unbearable monster, abusing the powers received from the gods, creating such chaos on earth that the gods had to remedy matters by sending down Vishnu to restore order, in his incarnation as Rama. Rama then becomes the sworn enemy of Ravana, and his crusade is the central motif of the *Ramayana* story.

- *Banteay Srei, N library pediment (20)*
- *Angkor Wat, corner pavilion*

The Invitation to the Descent of Vishnu The gods who invited Vishnu to incarnate as Rama were: Surya (the sun) on his chariot *(21)*, Soma (the moon) on a simpler chariot, Nirrti on the shoulders of a *yaksha*, Varuna, the god of water, riding a *naga (22)*, Brahma riding on his *hamsa* (sacred goose) *(23)*, Skanda riding the peacock *(25)*, Kubera (or Vayu) on his horse, Indra on his three-headed elephant Airavata *(24)*, Agni on his rhinoceros, Ketu (or Kubera) on his lion, Kalanemi, with seven heads visible *(26)*, Yama,

the god of justice on a chariot harnessed by buffaloes *(27)*, Shiva on a chariot pulled by two-humped bulls *(28)*.

- *Angkor Wat, NW corner pavilion, and N Gallery, W wing (Devas & Asuras)*

Rama's Archery Contest (Book 1, *Bala Kanda*) The childhood of Rama, his upbringing at Ayodhya and his learning of magic spells from a hermit, are not shown in any reliefs. The first event illustrated occurs when he has reached marrying age and participates in an archery contest. The scene occurs at the court of King Janaka who wishes to find a husband for his daughter Sita, and has organised a series of trials for the aspiring suitors.

In the original Valmiki text (Book 1, *Bala Kanda*), the main trial involved lifting and bending the unrivalled magic bow that King Janaka inherited from King Devarata. As was to be expected, Rama not only raised the bow with one hand, but effortlessly bent it. His strength was such as to break the bow in two, with a clap of thunder, dazzling and stunning the surrounding people.

The Khmer version is different. As seen in the reliefs, Rama wins by shooting a bird with an arrow through a turning wheel at the top of a mast.

Subsequently, the marriage of Rama with Sita is celebrated.

- *Angkor Wat, NW corner pavilion (29)*

Sita's abduction by the *rakshasa* Viradha (Book 3, *Aranya Kanda*) Rama, Lakshmana and Sita were wandering in the dense Dandaka forest when they came face to face with a monster as large as a mountain, creating great uproar, and causing the earth to tremble. It was Viradha, the son of Java and Shatarada. In an episode prefiguring Sita's abduction by Ravana, he managed to grab Sita, but while carrying her like a baby and trying to devour her, was transfixed with arrows by Rama and Lakshmana. Badly wounded he continued to fight, roaring and bursting into loud laughter, while still attacking the two brothers. Rama shot

*20 Ravana shaking Mount Kailasa. Banteay Srei.
(Photo: M. Freeman)*

*21 Surya, the Sun god, on a chariot drawn by four horses.
Angkor Wat, N gallery, W wing. (Photo: J. Poncar)*

22 Varuna, the god of water, mounted on a naga.
Angkor Wat, N gallery, W wing. (Photo: J. Poncar)

23 Brahma on hamsa, *holding the magic weapon*
brahmastra. *Angkor Wat, N gallery, W wing.
(Photo: J. Poncar).*

*24 Indra on Airavata with four tusks and holding an enemy.
Angkor Wat, N gallery, W wing. (Photo: J. Poncar)*

*25 Skanda, the god of war, on his peacock. Angkor
Wat, N gallery, W wing. (Photo: J. Poncar)*

two powerful arrows which cut the shining spear of Viradha in half. Despite this, the monster grabbed them and fought on until he was struck by the innumerable arrows and sword blows of the two heroes. At this point, they started to dig a pit to bury him, until he spoke revealing he was Gandharva Tumburu, who had incurred the wrath of Kubera for having loved the nymph Rambha. Since the monster could not be killed by weapons, they buried him in the ground. Finally he was dead; Rama and Lakshmana rejoiced and Sita was free.

• *Banteay Srei, main shrine* (**30**)

Rama killing Tataka (Book 3, *Aranya Kanda*) During their wanderings, Rama and Lakshmana reached a dark forest where a *rakshasa* woman (a *rakshini*) was spreading terror and death. She was Tataka, mother of Marica, stronger than a thousand elephants, who could change her form at will. After being ordered by the sage Vishvamita to kill her, Rama promised also to cut off her ears and nose. While he was speaking, however, Tataka attacked him, creating confusion with her magic tricks. Rama cut off both her hands, and Lakshmana her nose and ears; but since the monster was still fighting, Rama had to kill her with a single shaft in the heart. He was praised by Indra.

This interpretation, based on the *Ramayana*, is proposed by some scholars for the two personages on a small relief from Banteay Srei, which is considered here to represent Shiva (as a *kirata* or hunter) and Arjuna fighting hand to hand, in the dispute over who had been the first to shoot and kill a boar (see page 91).

• *Banteay Srei* (**129**, *page 91*)

Rama killing Marica (Book 3, *Aranya Kanda*) In the depths of the forest inhabited by ascetics, where Rama was in exile with his wife and brother Lakshmana, he saw a golden gazelle into which the *rakshasa* Marica had transformed on the order of Ravana. Marica was the son of a *yaksha* (a semi-divine being) and had became, through a curse, a *rakshasa*. Rama shot the arrow and wounded the gazelle, which, while dying, assumed the original shape of a huge *rakshasa*. This confrontation caused Rama to be distracted, thus allowing Ravana to abduct Sita.

• *Angkor Wat, SW corner pavilion* (**19**, *page 31*)

The abduction of Sita by Ravana (Book 3, *Aranya Kanda*) Ravana, infatuated by the beauty of Sita, decided to seize her. After distracting Rama and his brother by impelling them to hunt a golden gazelle Marica (see above), he achieved his objective of approaching Sita in a hermitage, in the guise of an ascetic. Having been rejected, he assumed his original terrible shape "resembling death itself", with ten heads and 20 arms. He grasped her, ascended in his magic chariot and rose high in the sky towards Lanka, while the overpowered Sita, struggling in distress, was crying loudly for her beloved Rama.

• *Banteay Srei, long room close to Gopura II E* (**17**, *page 28*)

The killing of Kabandha (Book 3, *Aranya Kanda*) During their wanderings in the forest, Rama and Lakshmana met Kabandha, a fearsome monster without a head but with a face on his stomach instead, who grabbed them in an attempt to devour them. However, they escaped by killing the monster. The relief at Angkor Wat shows the two heroes brandishing swords, in contrast to the Valmiki texts which indicates the use of bow and arrows.

• *Bapuon, Gopura II*
• *Angkor Wat, NW corner pavilion* (**31**)

Rama and Lakshmana comforting Sugriva (Book 3, *Aranya Kanda*) The brothers continued to wander in the forest without their beloved Sita. Having reached Mount Malaya, they noticed, below a tree, a monkey in deep sorrow. It was the king of the monkeys, Sugriva, dethroned by his brother Valin, and expelled from the kingdom.

• *Bapuon, Gopura II* (**32**)

26 Kalanemi, with seven heads visible. Angkor Wat, N gallery, W wing. (Photo: J. Poncar)

27 Yama, the god of justice, follows on a chariot harnessed by buffaloes. Angkor Wat, N gallery, W wing. (Photo: J. Poncar)

28 Shiva on a chariot pulled by two-humped bulls. (Photo: J. Poncar)

29 Rama's archery contest, Angkor Wat, NW corner pavilion. (Photo: EFEO)

30 The abduction of Sita by the rakshasa *Viradha. Banteay Srei, main shrine. (Photo: M. Freeman)*

31 The killing of Kabandha. Angkor Wat, NW corner pavilion.(Photo: EFEO)

Alliance of Rama and Sugriva (Book 4, *Kishkindha Kanda*) After Rama and Lakshmana had commiserated with Sugriva they decided to establish an alliance. In exchange for helping Sugriva to regain the throne, he would help them to reach Lanka with an army of monkeys, fight Ravana and regain Sita.

- *Banteay Srei, pediment from Gopura II W*
- *Bapuon, Gopura II N (33)*
- *Angkor Wat, NW corner pavilion (over the door)*

The duel between Sugriva and Valin – the killing of Valin (Book 4, *Kishkindha Kanda*) Because of his pact, Rama had to guarantee the victory of Sugriva over his brother Valin, by shooting the latter down with an arrow in an ambush, while the brothers were engaged in a hand-to-hand fight. Valin died in the arms of his wife Tara, amongst grieving monkeys.

- *Banteay Srei, pediment from Gopura II W (Phnom Penh Museum) (41)*
- *Bapuon, Gopura II N*
- *Angkor Wat, SW corner pavilion*

Hanuman meeting Sita (Book 5, *Sundara Kanda*) After so many vicissitudes, Sugriva summoned his soldiers and sent them in search of Sita. The group, led by the white monkey general Hanuman, managed to reach Sita, held prisoner in Lanka, in an acacia bush. He gave her Rama's ring as a sign of his commitment to get her back.

- *Bapuon, Gopura II (35)*
- *Angkor Wat, NW Corner pavilion*

Rama's alliance with *Vibhishana* (Book 6, *Yuddha Kanda*) To further ensure his success in rescuing Sita, Rama entered into an alliance with the *rakshasa* Vibhishana, who had been betrayed by his brother Ravana.

- *Angkor Wat, NW Corner pavilion*

Kumbhakarna (Book 6, *Yuddha Kanda*) According to Giteau (1955), Kumbhakarna was one of the sons of the *rakshasa* king of Lanka, born of Ravana and Vibhisana. Although he occupied a minor position in the *Ramayana* myths of the Angkorean period in the Valmiki tradition, he assumed greater importance in the *Ramakerti* of the 16-17th centuries, when he became the protagonist of one of the greatest fights preceding the Battle of Lanka. He was big, always sleepy, and a glutton. Two episodes of his life are represented in the reliefs of Bapuon temple:

Kumbhakarna waking up The *rakshasa* is represented in deep sleep while the monkeys attempt to wake him by beating drums, hitting his head, prodding him with a stick, and getting a small elephant to nudge him (*36*).

Kumbhakarna fighting He is represented wide-awake, amongst a storm of monkeys (*Yuddha Kanda*, *surga* LXVI) sent against him by Lakshmana, which he eventually grabs by their limbs and catapults into the air or devours. He was known to be able to eat monkeys by the dozen, while walking (*37*).

- *Bapuon, Gopura II W, E face*

The Battle of Lanka – Rama killing Ravana (Book 6, *Yuddha Kanda*) Finally, a long fierce battle takes place at Lanka, with fluctuating fortunes for the two adversary armies, until Rama manages to kill Ravana in single combat.

- *Angkor Wat, W Gallery, N wing (where the two protagonists are far apart) Also in pediments of the second courtyard, (39)*
- *Many other temples, including Preah Khan*

Indrajit and Lakshmana (Book 6, *Yuddha Kanda*) Four chapters of the *Yudda Kanda* tell the story of the battle between Lakshmana and Indrajit (sometimes known as Meganadha), Ravana's son. He is the one that wounded Lakshmana with magic arrows in the forehead, causing him to fall into a coma. However, Sushena, a powerful monkey leader (father of Tara, Valin's wife) "administered a sovereign remedy to the nostrils of Lakshmana and had him liberated from his darts and wounds". In some reliefs, Sushena is seen together with other monkeys in the act of bringing pieces of a mountain with the miraculous herbs used for the medicament.

*32 Rama and Lakshmana comforting Sugriva.
Bapuon, Gopura II N.*

*33 Alliance of Rama and Sugriva.
Angkor Wat, NW corner pavilion.*

34 Sita's ordeal by fire. Bapuon, Gopura II, E face.

35 Hanuman meeting Sita. Bapuon, Gopura II.

36 Kumbhakarna sleeping. Bapuon, Gopura II W.

37 Kumbhakarna fighting the monkeys. Bapuon, Gopura II W.

• *Angkor Wat, pediment facing the surrounding court of the 2nd level* (**41**)

Rama entering Ayodhya (Book 6, *Yuddha Kanda*) At last, on the magic chariot Pushpaka harnessed by geese, stolen by Ravana from Kubera, Rama returned triumphant, together with his followers, to his city where he would be crowned king.

• *Angkor Wat, NW corner pavilion (badly preserved)*

Sita's ordeal by fire (Book 7, *Uttara Kanda*) After so much struggle Sita is returned to Rama, but with a complication: Rama refuses to take her with him because she had been too long in the palace of Ravana and he suspects infidelity. "I have freed you" says Rama, brutally adding: "but you cannot be anymore mine because Ravana has abused you". In reality, during her long time of imprisonment, Ravana never touched her. Sita protests her innocence, but Rama forces her to withstand the proof of fire on a stake.

• *Angkor Wat, NW corner pavilion (very badly preserved)*

• *Bapuon, E Gopura II, E face* (**34**)

39 *The Battle of Lanka. Angkor Wat, pediment from Second courtyard.*

40 *Indrajit and Lakshmana. Angkor Wat, pediment from Second courtyard.*

Opposite: **41** *The duel between Sugriva and Valin. The killing of Valin. Banteay Srei, pediment from Gopura II W. (Photo: M. Freeman)*

THE KRISHNA MYTHS

GENERAL

The *Harivamsa* – a later appendix of the *Mahabharata* – deals mainly with the mythological adventures of Shiva and Vishnu. The latter appears in his divine incarnation as Krishna, and sometimes in human incarnation as Rama. From this text the Khmer took only some specific episodes, usually the great cosmic battles between *devas* and *asuras*, good and evil. In Khmer reliefs Krishna is commonly shown on the shoulders of Garuda, the winged divinity and enemy of the *asuras* and of *nagas*. Stories of the infancy of Krishna are centred around his uncle Kamsa who wanted to kill him, and began with a massacre of young children. No pastoral scenes are known.

THE CHOICE OF THEMES

Vishnu sleeping on the snake Ananta

(The *Harivamsa*). The god is represented reclining on the mythical *naga* Ananta, here shown in the form of a dragon, floating on the Ocean of Milk, sleeping between two cosmic eras. This attitude is known as *Anantasayin*.
  • *Preah Khan (42)*

Vishnu in the battle between the *Devas* and the *Asuras* (The *Harivamsa*)

All the great gods of the Hindu pantheon and the lesser divinities (*devas*), with their classic attributes, riding their traditional mounts, joined battle with the evil *asuras*. Taking part in this contest were Kubera, the god of wealth; Skanda, the god of war on his traditional mount, the peacock; Indra on Airavata, the elephant; Vishnu on his intrepid Garuda; Yama, on a chariot pulled by oxen; Shiva throwing the arc, or trident; Brahma riding his *hamsa*; Surya, the sun god; Varuna, the god of water, who appears mounted on a *naga*.
  • *Angkor Wat, N gallery, W wing (43)*

Vishnu's incarnation as a dwarf (The *Puranas*)

The story starts with King Bali becoming too powerful, due to his multiple austerities and meditation. He had earned such great merit that Indra felt threatened by him, and thus asked Vishnu for help. Vishnu agreed to be incarnated as the dwarf Vamana (his fifth *avatar*), and visited Bali to beg from him for the amount of land he could encompass in three-and-a-half strides. Bali, in his pride, laughed at the dwarf's foolishness, and granted the wish. Vishnu then expanded himself to such an extent that he measured the entire earth with his first step, heaven with the second, and the underworld with the third. He still required half a step more, which the king could not provide, and his pride was thus extinguished. Vishnu then stepped on Bali to claim the half step, and thus brought about the king's end.
  • *Angkor Wat, Preau Cruciform*
  • *Preah Pithu, monument 'y' (44)*

Krishna's infancy (*Bhagavad Purana*)

When still a little boy, Krishna was gifted with enormous strength, and, while in the cradle, strangled monsters sent to him by his uncle, King Kamsa. It had been predicted to the latter that he would be dethroned and assassinated by a new-born nephew, the eighth child born of his cousin Devaki (*Harivamsa*). As a consequence, King Kamsa, a latter-day Herod, ordered the massacre of all young boys, Krishna was exchanged with another child, a little girl, and managed to survive being smashed against a rock (*133*, page 93). Later, Kamsa renewed his efforts to kill his nephew by sending a furious elephant to charge at him. Krishna, holding the animal tightly by the tail, catapulted it into space. Finally, as might be expected, the wicked Kamsa was killed by the one he wanted to kill, and his body was parted in two by the powerful fist of the god.
  • *Bapuon, Gopura II, S face,*
  (45, 133 page 93)

42 Vishnu sleeping on the snake Ananta. Preah Khan. (Photo: M. Freeman)

44

43 Vishnu in the battle of the devas *and* asuras.
Angkor Wat, N gallery, W wing. (Photo: J. Poncar)

44 The three steps of Vishnu. Preah Pithu, temple 'y'.

45 Krishna's infancy. Bapuon, Gopura II, S face.   *45*

Krishna uprooting the *arjuna* trees (*Bhagavad Purana*) While still a young boy, Krishna was so restless that his adoptive mother Yasoda (wife of Nanda the cowherd) bound him with a rope to a heavy stone mortar. Such was Krishna's strength that he managed to move and, while dragging the mortar, uprooted two large trees.

- *Bapuon*
- *Angkor Wat, SW corner pavilion (46)*
- *Banteay Samre (Giteau)*

Krishna killing the *naga* Kaliya (*Bhagavad Purana*) A pool of the Kalindi river was infested by *nagas*, of which the most poisonous was Kaliya. Cattle and cow-herds who drank the polluted water to relieve their thirst, all fell lifeless on the pool banks. Observing the problem, Krishna incarnated as a young man, plunged into the virulent waters, but was soon enveloped by the coils of the *naga* and lay motionless. Seeing this, his friends and villagers became terrified and stupefied with grief. When Krishna saw how miserable his beloved people were, and how much they needed him, he escaped from Kaliya's grip, mounted on his head and smashed it by pounding his feet, in a sort of dance. Then, in his benevolence, Krishna told the wounded *naga* to leave for the ocean with all his group, and let the river be enjoyed by the herds and the people of the villages.

In Khmer reliefs, Krishna is represented in the action of splitting in two the six-headed *naga* Kaliya.

- *Bapuon, S Gopura II, S face (47)*
- *Banteay Srei*

Krishna killing King Kamsa (*Bhagavad Purana*) Krishna one day decided that the outrageous behaviour of Kamsa had gone too far and resolved to kill him, thus fulfilling the prophecy that the king would be killed by a member of his family. The *Harivamsa* text adds that another curse had been put on the king by the spirit of the little girl he had killed instead of Krishna. After being slain, she became an immortal, dreadful female consorting with bands of ghosts.

One night she spoke in fury to Kamsa announcing that, when overpowered and killed by his enemy (Krishna), she would smash his body with her own hands and drink his warm blood.

- *Banteay Srei (48)*

The Victory of Vishnu over the *asuras* (The *Harivamsa*) Once the elixir of immortality, the *amrita*, was obtained through the Churning of the Ocean of Milk, the *asuras* objected that they were excluded from sharing it, and attacked the *devas*. Another great battle took place, and Vishnu had to intervene, mounted, as usual, on Garuda, fighting against hosts of *asuras*, attacking him, alone, from both sides. Thanks to Garuda and to Vishnu's courage, victory was obtained, and Indra could be finally crowned king of the gods, and "rule with joy".

- *Angkor Wat, E gallery, N wing*

The Victory of Krishna over the *asura* Bana (The *Harivamsa*) The story is set against the background of a love story between the exceptionally beautiful daughter of Bana, Usha, and Aniruddha, Krishna's grandson (Bana was the son of the demon king Bali, a devotee of Shiva). To allow the two to marry, Usha's friend Chitralekha abducted Aniruddha, but Bana, enraged by the secret union of the two young people, sent his army to kill Aniruddha. A series of battles followed, and through illusionist and magic powers, Bana managed to capture Aniruddha who was bound with serpents and imprisoned in the fortified city of Shonitapura.

As a consequence, Krishna, launched a war against Bana. Before entering the city, Garuda extinguished the legendary 'five fires' (*49*). Then. Vishnu, riding on Garuda, and accompanied by his brother Balarama, got involved in close encounters on the battlefield. However, he met very strong resistance because Shiva was on the side of Bana; the two gods had fierce fights until Krishna hit Shiva with a special weapon, making him go to sleep. More fighting followed, during which Krishna, in one go, cut off the all but two of the one thousand arms of Bana. He was about

46 *Krishna uprooting the arjuna trees.*
Angkor Wat, SW corner pavilion. (Photo: EFEO)

47 *Krishna killing the six-headed naga Kaliya.*
Bapuon, S Gopura II, S face. (Photo: EFEO)

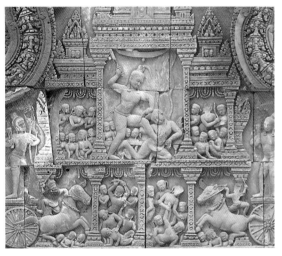

48 *Krishna killing King Kamsa. Banteay Srei. (Photo: M. Freeman)*

49 *Garuda extinguishing the five fires.*
Angkor Wat, N gallery, E wing. (Photo: J. Poncar)

50 *Krishna, with one thousand heads, paying respects to Shiva.*
Angkor Wat, N gallery, E wing.

51 *Detail of two Chinese women from*
Angkor Wat, E gallery, N wing. (Photo: J. Poncar)

to kill him when Shiva intervened, having previously promised immortality to Bana. Shiva said: "You, Krishna, are all-mighty in all nature; nobody can win against you. Be flexible, therefore. I have given my word to Bana and my word is not in vain". And Krishna answered: " Let him live, because you promised him safety! Because we are not distinct one from the other: what you are, I am."

This summarises the highest moral concepts of old Hindu religion: kingship, identity of all gods, all men and all beings. The battle ended with Aniruddha reunited with Usha.

> • *Angkor Wat, N Gallery*
> *Garuda extinguishing the five fires (49)*
> *Garuda, carrying Vishnu on his shoulder in the middle of the battle (54)*
> *Agni, with six heads and four arms mounted on a rhinoceros (52)*
> *Krishna, with 1,000 heads, paying respects to Shiva (50)*

Krishna's victory over the *asura* Narantaka
(The *Harivamsa*) This scene refers to Krishna winning a battle against the *asura* Narantaka who wanted to capture the sacred mountain of Mahiparvata.

> • *Angkor Wat, NW corner pavilion*

Krishna lifting Mount Govardhana
(The *Harivamsa*) The god is seen lifting the mountain above his head to protect the cowherds and their herds from the torrential rains caused by Indra's ire; he is accompanied by his brother Balarama. The god held the mountain above ground in one hand for seven days.

> • *Angkor Wat, SW corner pavilion.*
> • *Preah Khan*
> • *Banteay Samre (53)*

52 Agni, with six heads and four arms mounted on a rhinoceros. Angkor Wat, N gallery, W wing. (Photo: J. Poncar)

54 Opposite: Garuda, carrying Vishnu on his shoulder in the middle of the battle. (Photo: J. Poncar)

53 Krishna lifting Mount Govardhana. Banteay Samre. (Photo: M. Freeman)

55 *A statue of Vishnu in a temple. Bayon, Inner gallery.*

56 Shiva and Uma. Banteay Srei, S library. (Photo: M. Freeman)

THE SHIVA MYTHS

GENERAL

As mentioned above, the Shiva myths are rarely represented in Khmer reliefs.

Shiva became a sectarian God only in the late Epic age, in association with the worship of the *linga* and the cult of asceticism (*Mahabharata*, and *Puranas*). Before this time, he was assimilated with the Vedic god Rudra, (from the *Rig Veda* texts), and the pre-Veda phallic worship. In his rare appearances, he is usually represented as an ascetic, the images of him dancing *(Nataraja)* being quite rare in reliefs.

THE CHOICE OF THEMES

The myth of the *linga* (*Shiva Purana, Dharmasamhita*) This myth refers to the time when Brahma and Vishnu were arguing about which of them held the highest rank, and an immense column of fire appeared in front of them: it was the *linga* of Shiva, after he had castrated himself.

The two gods attempted to hold the extremities of the phallus, Brahma by flying up to the sky assuming the shape of a *hamsa* (goose) and Vishnu by digging down into the ground, transformed into a boar. Satisfied with this, Shiva appeared in the middle of the *linga*, with his many faces, arms, legs, resplendent with the light of the sun, moon and fire, and with the third eye. He disappeared after proclaiming the unity of Brahma, Vishnu and Shiva (*Maheshvara*), but his *linga* remained on earth. In this way the cosmic *linga* became the terrestrial *linga*.

This story is represented only in one relief sculptured on the lintel of Wat Eng Khna (7th century), where the *linga* is surrounded by stylised flames and has, at the front, the representation of Shiva's face. To its right, is Brahma and, to the left, Vishnu; in between them and the *linga* there are a *hamsa* and a boar.

 • *Wat Eng Khna (58)*

Shiva reducing Kama to ashes (*Saura Purana*) Kama, the god of love (known also as Madana, 'the one who brings madness'), is defined in the text as 'he who is born in the mind'. One day, he attempted to shoot an arrow made of flowers, or sugar, at Shiva in order to distract him from meditation. However, when Shiva, sitting close to Uma, saw this, he was furious, and reduced Kama to ashes by a ray from his frontal eye. After this, the god allowed a boon to Uma in distress, and she requested him to let Kama live and heat the world. Thus the god of love arose in an invisible form, to wander on earth like a wind, with his bow and arrow.

 • *Banteay Srei, S library, W pediment (57)*
 • *Angkor Wat, SW corner pavilion*

Shiva Bhikshatanamurti (probably from *Brahmanda Purana*) The appearance of a scantily dressed man in Khmer iconography has given rise to different interpretations. One relates him to the story of Shiva appearing naked in the pine forest, to test the self-control of the ascetics, stirred by jealousy of their wives. Another suggests that is Shiva from the incident when Shiva and Brahma argued about who was the real creator of the Universe, which impelled Shiva to murder a Brahmin. To expiate this sin, he had to become a beggar for 12 years, naked, as in all other interpretations, without even a loincloth (*bhikshtana murti*). In the Angkor relief, however, the young man is not represented naked – unthinkable in Khmer art – but wearing the smallest possible *sampot*.

Glaize (1944) proposed another interpretation, in which the figure may represent Ravana appearing as a handsome young man at the entrance of the chamber of Indra's wives, having sneaked through the door in the shape of a chameleon (or lizard).

The symbolism of the small reptile (chameleon, lizard, crocodile) that also appears in a few reliefs (Bayon, Kbal Spean) associated with Shiva, remains unexplained.

 • *Angkor Wat, SW corner pavilion*
 • *Bayon, S Inner (59) and N Inner galleries*

57 Shiva reducing Kama to ashes. Banteay Srei, S library. (Photo: M. Freeman)

*59 Shiva Bhikshatanamurti.
Bayon, Inner N gallery, W wing.*

58 Detail showing the myth of the linga.
Wat Eng Khna. (Photo: EFEO)

Shiva disturbing Parvati in meditation

(*Kumarasambhava*, one of many *Puranas*)
When, one day, Parvati was making penance in order to become worthy of her husband, the god himself, in the semblance of a coarse ascetic, tried to distract her by imprecating against Shiva. Parvati resisted the outrage by plugging her ears with her fingers. She was eventually rewarded by Shiva, who, after revealing himself, admitted having tried to test her fidelity.

 • *Unknown temple from the Preah Pithu complex, now in Musée Guimet (60)*

Arjuna and the *kirata* (*Mahabharata*)
Arjuna appears as an ascetic and a valiant warrior who had the task of re-establishing order on earth. Pandu, his real father, chose Indra as his 'godly' father, to make him gifted with divine power but still retain his humanity. To be acknowledged as the son of Indra, Arjuna had to go through asceticism and penance, during which he was involved in a fight with a *kirata* (whose form Shiva had adopted) over who had been the first to hit with an arrow a wild boar. The boar in Hindu symbolism represents sacrifice (Rodriguez, 1966); his legs are the *Vedas*, his tusks sacrificial blades, and his tongue Agni. The demon Muka, metamorphosed as a boar with the intention of killing Arjuna, became the sacrificial animal.

Arjuna, having lost his magic weapons and his power during the fights against the *kirata*, also represents sacrifice, and when he enters into a man to man combat with Shiva, his vulnerability and sacrifice are emphasised.

Then the *kirata* reveals his divine identity as Shiva and consecrates Arjuna as king by returning his weapons and giving him the absolute weapon, so that he can re-establish the *dharma*. Arjuna thus incarnates both royalty given legitimacy by a god, and has a semi-divine status, two aspects highly appreciated by Khmer kings.

At Banteay Srei the scene is represented by a single boar depicted frontally, and two archers placed symmetrically to the central scene, representing Arjuna and Shiva in combat. At Bapuon the story is shown in a series of

superposed panels, with the duel on the East face of Gopura II East, and the gift of weapons on the West face of Gopura II West (*61*).

 • *Banteay Srei, Central shrine (129, page 91)*
 • *Bapuon, Gopura II (61)*
 • *Prasat Sen Kev*
 • *Bayon, N Inner gallery, E wing*

61 The Arjuna's penance. Bapuon, Gopura II.

60 Shiva disturbing Parvati. From Preah Pithu, now in the Musée Guimet. (Photo: M. Freeman)

INDRA MYTHS

The mythology of Indra, the god of gods, goes back to the *Rig Vedas*, the earliest Indian texts (1,200 BC), in which, however, no specific myths are narrated, but are simply alluded to or vaguely mentioned. Our knowledge is thus derived from later reworked editions of the *Vedas* and their commentaries, in addition to myths described in other texts, like the *Mahabharata* and *Ramayana*.

There was no cult uniquely devoted to the god Indra in Khmer religion. He must have been, however, one of the most popular gods since he was also the god of heavens, of the sky, and in control of the fertilising rains. Moreover, he was the warrior of the gods and the protector of heroes, images that the kings desired to emulate. He was also one of the four main gods of direction (*lokapalas*), being the god of the East, and in Khmer temples he is repeatedly represented on door lintels and small pediments above the eastern entrances. In these manifestations, he is shown in human form sitting or standing on his mount, the famous three-headed elephant Airavata (*63*).

Gods ruling the three other main directions were Yama, King of the ancestors and the dead in charge of the South; Varuna, Lord of the waters, in charge of the West; and Kubera, Lord of wealth, men and genii, in charge of the North. There were also gods for the intermediate directions: Agni for the South East, Surya for the South West, Vayu for the North West and Soma for the North East.

One Indra myth particularly favoured by the Khmers was:

The rain of Indra One day, the great King Indra on his elephant, was asked by men to terminate the drought on earth, and so he did by unleashing a torrential rain, to the great rejoicing of all living beings.

• *Banteay Srei, S library (62)*

62 *The rain of Indra. Banteay Srei, S library. (Photo: M. Freeman)*

63 *Indra is usually on Airavata. Banteay Srei.*

OTHER HINDU MYTHS

The Churning of the Ocean of Milk (Although this story is also told in the *Mahabharata*, it is in the *Bhagavad Purana* that it is most complete).

The legend starts at the beginning of the world, when the *devas* and *asuras*, fought bitterly between themselves for 1,000 years in an effort to produce the *amrita*, an elixir that would render them immortal.

After some time, when they were tired and unable to achieve their goal, they asked the help of Vishnu. He appeared and ordered them to work together, not against each other. They agreed and organised themselves, the *asuras* to the left headed by three generals, with Bali holding the snake's head, and the *devas* to the right commanded by a general with an unusual head-dress, Lord Shiva (with five faces), and, at the end, holding the tail of the *naga*, the mighty monkey king Sugriva.

They started then to churn the Ocean of Milk by using Mount Mandara as the pivot. However, this suddenly started to sink. Vishnu intervened in his incarnation as the tortoise Kurma, and offered the back of his shell as a support for the mountain. The divine serpent Vasuki, with five heads, offered himself as the rope and curled himself around the pivot, which many gods, including Indra, helped to keep in position. The spinning of Mount Mandara created such a violent whirlpool that the mythological creatures and fish around it were torn to pieces in great numbers.

The Ocean of Milk was churned for another 1,000 years before producing the much-desired elixir and other treasures including the goddess Lakshmi (Sri Devi), the elephant Airavata, the horse Uccaishrava, a wishing tree, and the *apsaras*. A bitter confrontation took place between the *devas* and the *asuras* as to who would have the *amrita*, and another great battle took place. Vishnu had to intervene again, and with the help of the *devas*, won the battle and gained possession of the *amrita* which he kept out of harm's way. Once peace was established, Indra was reinstalled as the king of the gods. In Khmer mythology this act was very significant, since it could be related to the peaceful installation of the king of the Khmers.

According to the text, the *naga* Vasuki, with five heads full of fangs, vomited floods of blue venom due to his mishandling by the *devas* and *asuras*. This would have been enough to poison everybody, had it not been for Shiva, who drank it all, his mouth remaining stained with a black line forever as a result. However, this episode is not part of Khmer iconography.

- *Angkor Wat, E gallery, S wing (**64**)*
- *Angkor Wat, SW corner pavilion*
- *Banteay Srei*
- *Banteay Samre*

Heavens and Hells There is no hell in Hindu mythology. Therefore, the concept of life after death (a rare motif in Khmer art), of the last judgement, and the resulting joy in heaven in contrast to the torments of hell, must originate from Mahayana Buddhist beliefs. The number 32 of existing hells is significant only in Buddhist numerology. This is a further demonstration of the instinctive syncretism of the Khmers.

In their mythological vision of heaven and hell, a particularly impressive figure must have been that of Yama, the God of Judgement (**65**), and sovereign of the nether regions. According to tradition, he has a grim appearance, ugly, with dark green skin, glowing red eyes and long teeth. Usually riding a buffalo, he is dressed in blood-red garments, has a crown, and carries an axe, a sword, and a dagger.

At death, when the soul leaves the body, Yama's assistant Dharmma (**66**) brings the deceased, along with his/her deeds, in front of the record keeper, Citragupta; sentence is pronounced before the throne of Yama, who appears indulgent to the just, but terrible towards the sinners. Although the embodiment of righteousness (*dharma*) and the king of Justice (*dharma-raja*), he feels no pity (Danielou, 1985). The damned, after passing through the southern gate with a red-hot iron grid, and across a fetid

64 The Churning of the Ocean of Milk. Vishnu on Mount Mandara, supported by the turtle. Angkor Wat, E gallery, S wing. (Photo: J. Poncar)

65 Yama. Heavens and Hells. Angkor Wat, S Gallery, E wing. (Photo: J. Poncar)

66 Dharmma and Citragupta from Heavens and Hells. Angkor Wat, S Gallery, E wing. (Photo: J. Poncar)

boiling river, are thrown into a hell inhabited by dreadful monsters, where they are subjected to the most inventive and terrible forms of torture. (*68-70*).

The concept of hell is in contradiction with that of reincarnation, but in Cambodia, as in India, the two mix happily together.

• *Angkor Wat, S gallery, E wing*

Tilottama story (The *Mahabharata*)
In order to put an end to the upheaval and desolation caused by the two *asuras* Sunda and Upasunda in the universe, the gods created the beautiful nymph Tilottama and sent her down with the mission to create a deadly rivalry between the two brothers. Tilottama is seen here being grabbed by each of the *asuras,* who, at the same time, raise heavy clubs to hit, and, hopefully, kill, each other. Two figures at each side of the main scene, are squatting, some praying. Two celestial beings (*devaputtas*) fly high in the sky, over the main tree of the forest.

• *Banteay Srei pediment, now at the Musée Guimet (67)*

68

69

67 *Tilottama and the* asuras. *Banteay Srei pediment, now Musée Guimet. (Photo: M. Freeman)*

70 *68-70 Various scenes from Hell, Angkor Wat, S gallery, E wing. (Photo: J. Poncar)*

EPIC BATTLES

The great epic battles of the *Ramayana* and *Mahabharata*, with 1,000s of protagonists (human, divine and evil), animals, chariots, all entangled in a dynamic melee, with clouds of flying arrows and spears, caught the imagination of the Khmer, who chose to represent them on the largest available surfaces. Thus the gallery of the Third Enclosure at Angkor Wat shows the battles of Kurukshetra, of Vishnu over the *asuras*, of Krishna against Bana, between *devas* and *asuras*, and, finally, the famous battle of Lanka (all considered above). Similarly, the legendary battles between the Khmers and the Chams at the time of Jayavarman VII, cover the majority of the exterior gallery of Bayon (see below).

The Battle of Kurukshetra (The *Mahabharata*)
This story, so popular in Khmer imagination, recounts the battle between the Pandavas and the Kauravas. In the Ganges Valley, at the heart of Northern India, Bishma, son of King Santanu, having taken the vow of celibacy, plots with his step-mother Satyavati to obtain heirs to the throne by inviting two girls to unite with the sage Vyasa, the son Satyavati had miraculously procreated before marrying Santanu. One child, born blind, became the great king Dhritarashtra, father of the Kauravas; the other, born very pale, became Pandu, later father of the five Pandava brothers, of whom the most famous is Arjuna.

Dhritarashtra, unhappy at occupying a place unsuitable to his infirmity, allowed his sons, grouped around the eldest, Duryodhama the nasty, to push their cousins, the five sons of Pandu, out of power. The old king Dhritarashtra had wanted to leave the kingdom to them. But his sons opposed this and through treachery arranged the exile of their rivals, denying them the smallest rights. Inevitably, war broke out.

The two families were great enemies, and the epic is symbolic of the conflict between the sons of Darkness (the Kauravas) and the sons of Light (the Pandavas). The ensuring bloodbath saw the annihilation of the flower of youth from the Feudal age of Vedic India. It is at this point in the

lengthy epic, that the *Bhagavad Gita* ('Song of the Lord') appears. When the young Arjuna refused to fight for a kingdom which would entail killing his own people, Krishna, acting as his charioteer (*71*), propounds the philosophy of *karma* to him, saying "your right is to do your *karma*, or duty, not to look for its result". Krishna pointed out that knowledge, work and devotion all lead to salvation. The battle of Kurukshetra was essential for the re-establishment of universal harmony.

A key personage in the story was the great lord Bishma (*72*), who had renounced the throne because of court intrigues, and, invincible due to his semi-divine origin, was able to choose the time of his death. He was on the Kauravas side. When, at the end of the 10th day, he lay wounded on a bed of arrows, he decided not to die till the sun had moved into the Northern hemisphere.

The battle raged for 18 days and nights, with endless acts of bravery and heroism. Exceptions to the laws of chivalry occur in the killing of Duryodhana by Bhima, of Karna by Arjuna, and the foul play of Yudhishthira towards Aswatthama. By the end of the eighteenth day, the Kaurava army was defeated, and the battle ended. Yudhishthira was crowned king and ruled for many years until he abdicated. Then, with his four brothers and their common wife Draupadi, he migrated to Mount Meru, in the Himalayan mountains, entering the realm of the gods.
• *Angkor Wat, W gallery, S wing (**71** and **72**)*

The duel between Bhima and Duryodhama (The *Mahabharata*) This is the fight between two protagonists of the battle of Kurukshetra, believed to be Bhima (of the Pandavas) and Duryodhama (of the Kauravas), in the presence of Krishna, who, with his four arms, helps his brother Balarama to hold his favourite weapon, the *phkak* (long-handled club ending at an angle with two blades). During the fight, one of the combatants leaps over his adversary to hit him with a lethal blow. The *apsaras*, the usual witnesses of mythical scenes, fly around above the duel with dancing gestures.
• *Banteay Srei pediment, now at the Phnom Penh museum (**73**)*

71 *Krishna acts as charioteer for Arjuna in the Battle of Kurukshetra. Angkor Wat, W gallery, S wing. (Photo: J. Poncar)*

72 *The death of Bishma. Angkor Wat, W gallery, S wing. (Photo: J. Poncar)*

73 *The duel between Bhima and Duryodhama. Banteay Srei pediment, now Musée Guimet. (Photo: M. Freeman)*

BUDDHIST MYTHS

INTRODUCTION

Sculptural reliefs narrating Buddhist stories of
any kind are rare in the historical period under
consideration, for two reasons. Firstly, few
Buddhist stone temples were built before
Jayavarman VII. Secondly, those built by
Jayavarman VII had their Buddhist reliefs largely
destroyed by the iconoclasm following his death.
It seems that the defacement was directed against
the Mahayana icons in the temples he had
erected, and specifically against the icons of the
Buddha. Many Bodhisattvas escaped because they
could easily be assimilated to the figure of Shiva.

   On the contrary, Theravada temples and their
images were spared. A possible explanation is that
Theravada Buddhism had been tolerated since
the reign of Yashovarman I, who allowed the
building, towards the end of the 9th century, of
Tep Pranam, a terrace with a large Buddha statue,
in the shade of the Royal palace.

   However, in the present state of knowledge,
there are doubts about the dating of many of the
reliefs on the temples prior to the time of
Jayavarman VII, and it seems evident that some
were added in the 16th century.

   The main question that arises from research
into Khmer mythology based on the narrative
reliefs is: how did Jayavarman visually express his
devotion to Buddhism?

   It seems mostly to have been manifested
through architectural symbolism, primarily in
three colossal building complexes: the huge
monastery-temple of Ta Prohm, run by 12,640
people, and dedicated to Prajñaparamita, for the
king's mother; the monastery-university-temple of
Preah Khan, supported by more than 97,000
people, with a Lokeshvara statue at its centre in
the semblance of the king's father, and finally,
Bayon, a pantheon of Buddhist, Shivaite and
Vishnuite divinities and local genies, crowned by
more than 200 colossal heads of Lokeshvara
(assuming that they are not of Brahma). Bayon
combines Hindu symbolism (Mount Meru, the
Churning, the *naga* bridge between earth and sky)
with Buddhist cosmology (the Hall of Good

74 Buddha under Naga. *National Museum, Bangkok.*
(Photo: M. Freeman)

Order, Sudhammasabha), and possibly also evokes
a *mandala* with the Buddha protected by the *naga*
at the centre.

   To these should be added many more temples
dedicated to the Buddhist faith: to mention only a
few, Banteay Chhmar, Banteay Kdei, Ta Nei, Ta
Som, the Neak Pean basin charged with
Mahayana symbolism, and more than 100
'hospitals'. In them, Buddhist stories appear only
sporadically.

   It has not been possible to study the reliefs
from Banteay Chhmar in person (inaccessible at
the time of this research), nor those of Preah
Khan of Kompong Svay. It was also decided not
to include the Buddhist temples in North-east
Thailand such as Phimai in order to keep the
book of manageable size.

   Regrettably, the scenes from the *Vessantara*

Jataka that Glaize (1993) reported as existing at Banteay Samre have not been studied. In the Phnom Penh Museum, a stone fragment reputed to be from the 'West entrance of Angkor Wat' (No.1701), allegedly depicts scenes from the *Vessantara Jataka* but its reading, on three short vertical panels, is quite problematic. It is dated to the end of 12th-early 13th century.

It is surprising that in all these numerous important buildings, there are so few narrative reliefs relating to Buddhism, or dealing with the life of Buddha, particularly the *jatakas*. The *Vessantara*, so widespread in Southeast Asia, was sparingly used by the Khmers, even though it was preferred over other *jatakas* for its analogy with the *Ramayana*.

Although Jayavarman VII emulated the grand decorative tradition of his predecessors, as far as the narrative reliefs of his own temples are concerned, he had the outer gallery of Bayon decorated with large panels narrating his earthly exploits, his battles against the enemies of Cambodia, without any reference to Buddhism. The inner gallery reliefs of later date were sculpted by his successors of Brahmanic faith, who obviously avoided Buddhist iconography.

In conclusion, although it is more than evident that Jayavarman demonstrated his Mahayana faith by building a record number of large monuments charged with religious symbolism, he left a comparatively small number of iconographic narrative representations, possibly in accordance with the Tantric orientation of Mahayana of that time.

From the 14th century, Theravada gradually replaced Mahayana Buddhism, as the most popular religion in Cambodia. When, in the 16th century Angkor was reoccupied, a new Buddhist fervour arose, and some older Buddhist temples were expanded, sometimes with the addition of *stupas*. New reliefs were carved, and a general refurbishment, mainly in wood, was completed. The same applies to some provincial temples.

Although this book concentrates on the Angkorean period, later myths and legends are considered, in view of the scarcity of Buddhist narrative material.

THE CHOICE OF THEMES

As they had done in the case of Hindu mythology, the Khmers again exercised a very individual choice of events, portraying a particularly narrow selection of stories from the life of Buddha. There are no representations of Siddhartha's conception and birth, so common in Indian and Indonesian iconography. Also, the stories relating to his early years, the pivotal Four Encounters, the First Sermon and other scenes of his teaching, and the Descent from Heaven, are all missing from Khmer narrative relief sculptures, although they were widely portrayed by other cultures of Southeast Asia.

The following events have been recognised from Khmer narrative reliefs of the 6th to the 16th centuries.

The sleep of women This refers to the last night spent by the Buddha-to-be in his royal house, surrounded by the court ladies and dancers, whom the gods plunged into a deep sleep. After giving his wife and son a last glance, the Future Buddha will secretly leave the palace for good.
  • *Wat Nokor (76)*

The great departure This tells the story of the Future Buddha leaving his palace riding his horse Kanthaka, accompanied by his squire Chandaka, who holds the horse's tail. They are assisted by four celestial beings who support the horse's hoofs, making it possible to flee noiselessly. His father, King Shuddhodama has tried at all costs to prevent such an escape, but the gods have plunged all the town's inhabitants into a deep sleep, and had the town gates opened.
  • *Ta Prohm*
  • *Wat Nokor (77)*

The cutting of the hair After crossing the river Anoma, the Buddha-to-be, having renounced his princely attire and ornaments, decided to cut his hair, rejecting the privilege of his caste and choosing to follow the path of religious mendicants. Miraculously, his hair never grew again after this. The moment when he cuts a lock

75 The freeing of the horse and squire. Wat Nokor.

*78 The cutting of the hair. Detail of horse.
Monument X, Preah Pithu, now in
Conservancy of Siem Reap. (Photo: EFEO)*

77 Left: The Great Departure. Wat Nokor.

*76 Far left: The sleep of women.
Wat Nokor.*

of hair with his sword is one of the most popular events of Buddhist iconography.

• *Preah Pithu Monument 'x' (78)*

The freeing of the horse and squire
The Future Buddha, having dismounted from Kanthaka, his loyal horse, sets him free by cutting the bridles with a sword. The animal will die of sorrow, to be reborn in Indra's heaven.

• *Wat Nokor (75, see page 61)*

Buddha receiving the present of Sujata
After abandoning the life of absolute asceticism as useless, and having recovered his vitality, the Buddha-to-be began to beg for his subsistence like a monk. One day, while meditating under the 'tree of the goathherd' *(ajapala),* the young girl Sujata presented him with a golden bowl full of rice, believing he was the divinity of the tree to whom she had made a wish. Having divided this generous gift into 49 parts, one for each of the days he knew would be necessary to reach the Awakening, he threw the precious bowl into the river.

• *Preah Palilay (79)*

The attack of *Mara*
Mara was the god ruling over the World of Desire inhabited by ghosts, *asuras,* and animals, and knew that if the Future Buddha discovered the reason for the never-ending cycle of birth and rebirth, his power would come to an end.

Therefore, when *Mara* sees the Future Buddha in meditation under the *bodhi* tree, he decides to assault him, riding a war elephant, accompanied by an army of demons with animal faces. Unmoved by the ferocity of the devils, the Buddha puts *Mara's* army to flight through his superior spiritual power.

• *Wat Nokor (80)*
• *Prasat Chrap, Kompong Thom (pediment now at the Phnom Penh Museum, No.1824)*

Buddha's enlightenment
After the attack of *Mara,* the Future Buddha ascends to the highest level of meditation during which he reviews his former existence and the cycles of rebirth *(samsara)* which depend on *karma*. Perceiving the possibility of conquering birth and death, he is now certain of his deliverance. He comes into possession of the Four Noble Truths, and wakes up as a man of perception, an enlightened one. He has become a Buddha.

This culminating moment is commonly represented by the image of the Buddha seated under the *bodhi* tree in the *bhumisparsa mudra,* left hand in his lap and right hand touching the ground, and the *ushnisha* (cranial protuberance) on his head.

Occasionally this event is completed by reference to Brah Dharani, the Goddess of Earth, who responded to the Buddha's call to witness his enlightenment. She twists her hair to produce the flood of water that will drown the army of evil creatures that *Mara* has sent to destroy him.

• *Preah Palilay (81 and 82)*
• *Preah Khan*

Buddha on the *Naga* Muchalinda
In the sixth week of his enlightenment, the Buddha went to meditate close to a pond where dwelt the *naga*-king Muchalinda. When a thunderstorm arose, Muchalinda embraced the meditating Buddha with his body and protected him with his hood against the elements.

In Buddhist tradition, this prodigious event corresponds to the definitive attainment of Enlightenment, and is one of the most popular in Khmer art. Although very rare in sculptural reliefs, it is common in free-standing sculpture, particularly in the Bayon and post-Bayon period.

The miracle of the Parilyyaka Forest
Ten years after the enlightenment, the Buddha alone retired alone to the Parilyyaka forest, near Kosambi, where he was assisted and venerated by a lone elephant and a monkey. These two unfortunate beings, incapable of discerning good from evil, were to be reborn in the heaven of Indra, who taught them the way to salvation.

• *Preah Palilay (83, page 65)*

79 *Buddha receiving the present of Sujata. Preah Palilay.*

80 *The attack of Mara. Wat Nokor.*

81 and 82 *Buddha in meditation, Preah Palilay.*

Subjugation of Nalagiri 37 years after the Enlightenment, the Buddha's envious enemy, cousin Devadatta, decided to murder him by calling upon an elephant, Nalagiri, which he has intoxicated to madness. The animal is set loose in the street of Rajagriha, terrorizing the whole population, except for the Buddha. Nalagiri, moved by his benevolence, kneels at his feet and is immediately cured of his murderous intentions.

- *Preah Palilay (87)*

Attaining Mahaparinirvana The Buddha, having reached a garden near the town of Kushinagara, asks his assistant Ananda to prepare a bed between two sal trees. He lies down on his right side, facing west. Towards the end of the night, having completed the entire cycle of meditation, he attains Mahaparinirvana, and passes away. The earth shakes, gods appear and trees blossom. Mahaparinirvana is a state achievable only through extinction of the Self, eternal, beyond rationality.

- *Preah Palilay (84)*

Avalokiteshvara The most famous Bodhisattva of Buddhist iconography is Avalokiteshvara, 'The Lord of compassion', or 'The Lord that overlooks from above', who is always characterised by carrying a small image of Buddha Amitabha in his headdress.

In Cambodia he is better known as Lokeshvara, and is usually represented with four arms, carrying a lotus bud (thus the name *Padmapani*, carrier of lotus *padma*), a rosary, a water jar, and a manuscript. During the period of Jayavarman VII, particularly in free-standing sculpture, he is more commonly represented with eight arms, and assumes a cosmic meaning, with his body covered by a thousand small images of Buddha, emanating from each skin pore, radiating universal compassion.

- *Ta Prohm of Bati (85)*
- *Neak Pean, E face, false door of sanctuary (86)*
- *Neak Pean, W face, false door of central sanctuary*

The legend of the Balaha horse According to Bonheur (1989), this horse was the aspect assumed in a previous life by the Future Buddha, or – according to the Mahayana text of the *Karandavyuha Sutra* – the Bodhisattva Lokeshvara, in order to save the merchant Simhala and his companions from the danger into which they had fallen.

The Indian merchant Simhala and his compatriots, had sailed the seas in search of their fortune, but were shipwrecked and had to swim towards the isle of Lanka.

Unknown to them, the isle was the kingdom of ogresses, female monsters (*rakshini*, like in the *Ramayana*), who desired to capture men. Magically, in the evening, they would become beautiful to entice their victims, before regaining their real and horrible form later to devour them.

Miraculously informed of the danger, Simhala was in great distress for the lives of himself and his companions, when the horse Balaha appeared enabling them to reach 'the other shore', both materially and spiritually, As a result of this act, Balaha latter became the Buddha.

At Neak Pean, the legend is represented by a large free-standing statue within the pool surrounding the central sanctuary. Simhala and his companions are seen hanging on to the body, neck and tail of the large horse, who is swimming towards the sanctuary. The sad end of the story, however, is not represented. In fact, they did not reach salvation, as, having looked back to the ogresses (like in the Orpheus legend), and unable to resist their calls, they all perished except Simhala. He, later, returned with an army to Lanka to defeated the ogresses, pushing them back into the forest, and become king. He gave his own name to Sri Lanka, which is also called Simhaladvipa, the island of Simhala, and would be the future Buddha, according to the version of the *Karandavyuha Sutra*.

- *Neak Pean (88)*

83 The miracle of the Parilyyaka Forest. Preah Palilay.

84 Attaining Mahaparinirvana. Preah Palilay.

85 Avalokiteshvara. Ta Prohm of Bati.

86 Avalokiteshvara. Neak Pean.

88 The horse Balaha. Neak Pean. (Photo: M. Freeman)

87 Left: Subjugation of Nalagiri. Preah Palilay.

HISTORIC EVENTS

The best relief giving us an idea of what the army of King Suryavarman II might have looked like is that of the Southern Gallery, West wing of Angkor Wat, known as the 'Historic procession'. However, it is not clear if this was intended to represent an ordinary parade of the royal forces, or a particular ceremony.

It shows the entourage of the king, including Brahmin priests, recognisable by their high chignons, and the main state minister. The queens, princesses and ladies of the court are also represented. The sculptors have indicated the rank of the king by depicting the 14 parasols required by protocol, together with the complementary fly-whisks.

Then follows the parade of infantry, escorting the generals and high dignitaries mounted on elephants. A short inscription indicates the name and rank of each important personage, and the number of parasols conforms with it.

The relief gives an indication of the style of dress and the weapons of the army. The generals, as well as the infantry, have the lower body draped by a *sampot* whose long tails descend from the belt to drop on the side. The soldiers have helmets decorated with the head of an animal and carry a round shield. The horses of some chiefs are sculpted in great detail. In many cases, the king and the generals were conspicuously holding the *phkak*, the long-handled club ending at an angle in which two blades were inserted. This instrument is still used nowadays in Cambodia. It derives from Indonesia and is unknown in India.

The parade includes various groups of Brahmins, ringing small bells: the *Rajahota*, or royal priest, is carried in an hammock, just as in recent times. The propitious ark follows, containing the sacred fire escorting the army to sanctify the battle and attract the attention of the gods. The numerous porters are preceded by trumpets, drums, conch players, and an enormous gong beaten with a large mallet. Two dancing clowns are also depicted, and some banner-carriers juggling with their insignia (often a statuette of Hanuman). At the head of the procession, a group of unusual people appear: the Siamese, with extravagant costumes, long vests with pendants, bizarre hair-styles with three or four plumes and five rows of superimposed beads; their general is covered with bracelets and necklaces, plus many other decorative elements.

- *Angkor Wat, S gallery, W wing*
  (**89**, *a Khmer general*), (**90**, *youths*),
  (**91**, *soldiers and insignia*), (**92**, *a captain*)

Battles between Khmers and Chams Most of the early scholars have suggested that the battle scenes on the Outer gallery of Bayon represent real historical battles between Khmers and Chams. Boisselier (1993), was of the opinion that this may be only in part correct, as it was more likely that contemporary events were equated with scenes from ancient history and mythology, in particular battles between the *devas* and *asuras*. This would be a further reference to Indra's victorious battle against the *asuras*, so important for the symbolism of the gates of Angkor Thom. It was certainly more important to identify the career of Jayavarman VII, king of the Khmers, with that of Indra, king of the gods, than merely to commemorate contemporary events.

- *Bayon, Outer gallery*
  (**93**, *pages 68-69*), (**95**, *page 70*)
- *Bayon, Outer gallery*
  Naval Battles (**94**, *page 70*)

Scenes of daily life In the small narrative panels of Bapuon temple, legends, epic stories and scenes of daily life are mixed together, seemingly at random, without any definite order. Amongst them, a few mock the lives and weaknesses of ascetics, who are shown being pursued by a faun, churning milk, stripping a girl from her sarong, attempting to molest her, and practising some acrobatic yoga positions to gain merit. Other scenes are more dramatic: the ascetics are seen holding on their knees a decapitated head pierced by an arrow near a woman sitting between two executioners who are about to chop her head off.

*89 A general. Angkor Wat, S gallery, W wing.
(Photo: J. Poncar)*

*90 Some youths. Angkor Wat,
S gallery, W wing.*

*91 Vizajaya and Soldiers,
Angkor Wat, S gallery, W
wing. (Photo: J. Poncar)*

*92 A captain. Angkor Wat,
S gallery, W wing.
(Photo: J. Poncar)*

*93 Overleaf: Battle between
the Khmers and the Chams.
Bayon, Outer gallery.
(Photo: M. Freeman)*

94 *Naval battle between Khmers and Chams. Bayon, Outer gallery. (Photo: M. Freeman)*

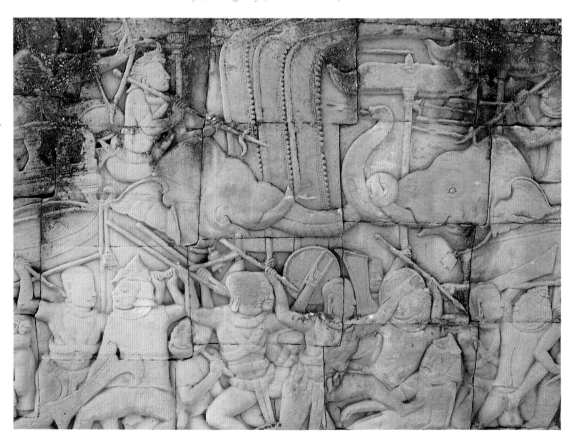

The outer gallery of Bayon is rich in reliefs illustrating stories and events of daily life with great verve. Some scenes depict the bank of a river (or lake) with boars in the bushes, together with flamingos, deer and does, intently watched by a hidden hunter. Not far away, Khmer warriors with straps crossed over their chests, prepare for battle and brandish their pikes.

Using the shore of the river bank to assure narrative continuity, the Bayon artists portray, in a lively and graphic way, open-air scenes – market stalls with buyers and sellers, cockfighting with the various punters in animated discussion, cooking, tending the sick, mothers and children, and so on.

Behind the market, fish swim close to boats in the river, along which there are houses and palaces, examples of the civil and rural architecture of the time, and inside which one can observe scenes of domestic life.

The reliefs depict boats and fishing equipment, including a curious anchor with a pulley, identical to those of Chinese junks. The fish themselves are the same as those found nowadays in the Great Lake and have all been identified.

For a better understanding of some of the scenes described in the reliefs of Bayon one can read the memoirs of Zhou Daguan, who visited Angkor in the late 13th century, and recorded a wealth of interesting facts.

"Every time I was admitted to the palace for an audience with the King, he came forward with his chief queen, and took his seat in the embrasure of the golden window in the main audience hall. The ladies of the court were drawn up on both sides of the veranda below the window, changing places now and then to get a better look at us, and thus giving me a good chance to see them".

"Finally the sovereign appeared, standing erect on an elephant and holding in his hand the sacred sword. This elephant, his tusks sheathed in gold, was accompanied by bearers of twenty white parasols with golden shafts. All around was a bodyguard of elephants, drawn together, and still more soldiers for complete protection, marching in close ranks".

"Every day the King holds two audiences for consideration of affairs of state. No list or agenda is provided. Functionaries and ordinary people who wish to see the sovereign seat themselves on the ground to await his arrival. In the course of time, distant music is heard in the palace, while from the outside blasts on conch shells sound forth as though to welcome the ruler." When the king enters the hall "All present, ministers and commoners, join their hands and touch the hearth with their foreheads, lifting up their heads only when the sound of conches has ceased. The sovereign seats himself at once on a lion's skin, which is a hereditary royal treasure. When the affairs of state have been dealt with, the king turns back to the palace, . . . everyone rises".

- *Bayon, Outer gallery (**97** and **98**)*
- *Angkor Wat, second courtyard.*

96 *Battle scene. Bayon, Outer gallery.*

95 *Opposite: Part of a battle scene between the Khmers and Chams. Bayon, Outer gallery.*

97 *and* **98** *Scenes of everyday life. Bayon, Outer gallery. (98 Photo: M. Freeman)*

Hunting scenes On the Terrace of the Elephants, different hunting scenes with elephants in the Cambodian forest are sculpted in deeper relief than usual. The action is shown in detail such as, when two elephants get hold of a tiger, or when they strangle a roebuck, while hunters are throwing spears at a boar, and a mahout drinks from his flask. Scenes of men hunting a tiger, and of hunters with a blow-pipe aiming at birds, are common at Bapuon temple.

  · *Terrace of the Elephants, Angkor Thom*
  · *Bapuon, Gopura II S*
  · *Bayon, Outer gallery (**99**)*

99 Hunting scenes. Bayon, Outer gallery. (Photo: J. Poncar)

Athletic games The athletic games at the time of Jayavarman VII, including horse riders fighting with spears, wrestlers, gladiators, and racing chariots, are well illustrated in the Elephant Terrace. The game of polo was also practised. It seems that these games were held by the king to entertain his aristocracy and courtiers, in the Royal square of Angkor Thom.

  · *Terrace of the elephants, Angkor Thom (**100** and **101**)*

101 100 and 101 Athletic games. Terrace of the Elephants, Angkor Thom. (Photo: M. Freeman)

100

MYTHOLOGICAL MOTIFS

Kala This mythological animal appears very frequently in Khmer reliefs (**107**, Wat Nokor). It is a monster with the head of a lion seen frontally, with two enormous bulging eyes, a grin showing the fangs. The *kala* head appears amongst the decorative scrolls and foliage, generally on the lintels above the doors. According to Hindu mythology it represents Shiva with a fierce menacing look, and is thus protective in nature, explaining its presence over doors to deter enemies and particularly the evil spirits always trying to enter the sanctuaries or sacred places. From a decorative point of view, this head is better known in Cambodia as the head of Rahu and occupies the centre of the lintels. It has a curious look in so far as its naturalistic character does not make concessions to the purely ornamental stylisation. From the open mouth frequently hangs a tongue which becomes part of the decoration. A unique peculiarity of the *kala*, is the absence of the lower jaw, and even more surprising, the presence on each side of the face, of two forearms, often reduced to two hands, holding the garlands exiting from its mouth. Perhaps, as Marchal has suggested (1955), this skull without jaw is reminiscent of the human skull that certain chiefs of Oceanic islands place at the top of their dwellings; the skull, on drying out, would loosen the lower jaw by breaking the ligaments. It is not only in Cambodia that certain motifs have lost their original magic and protective value, and have become mere decorative ornaments; similar examples occur in China (the stylised face of the 'T'ao tie' motif) and in the *kala* faces from India and Indonesia.

The original beliefs of local people required human sacrifices and the incorporation of the corpses in the structure of buildings, religious or civil. The magic power thus attributed to the monument would blend with the vital force diffused in the blood of the victims sacrificed to protect it. Khmer tradition indicates the existence of this tradition, and the *kala* is perhaps a visual embodiment of it. The head of a newly-sacrificed animal or human being was no longer incorporated into the masonry of the temple, but instead the head of a monster was sculpted over the entrance, charged with a propitiatory function.

Makara This is a bizarre hybrid being, resulting from a mixture of crocodile, fish, tapir, bird and elephant, stylised in a single figure which is interlaced with scrolls, volutes, vines and other ornaments. It is common in Khmer reliefs (**105**). In contrast to the *kala* and lion heads which are always represented facing the viewer, the *makara* is always seen in profile and occupies the edges of architectural elements such as the frame of a pediment, the ends of a lintel, etc. In general only the head is evident but sometimes the tail is directly attached to the head; the former often featuring a considerable extension, straightening up in the shape of scrolls and adopting a purely ornamental profile. From the open mouth with large fangs escapes either an animal, a small figure or the *naga*.

Apsaras and *devatas* These female figures assumed considerable importance in 12th and 13th century Khmer architectural decoration.

The *apsaras* are divine dancing girls, appearing in the skies of Khmer myths, while the *devatas* are divinities of Indra's paradise, usually framed in a flaming arch (**102**, page 76). These delightful beings bring a special charm to the religious ambience of the temple, which is otherwise rather severe: they are always bare-breasted, adorned only with jewels, and with elaborate hairstyles.

Naga and *Garuda* The *naga* is a serpent-god of the waters, living underground or in water, with a cobra hood and many heads, normally seven or nine in number. From early times, it was the mythological protagonist of the legend concerning the origin of the Khmer people, when a Indian Brahmin married a *naga*-princess by the name of Soma, thus founding the first local royal dynasty.

The *naga* is the guardian of the treasure of the earth, the keeper of the energy stored in water, and the safeguarder of the prosperity of the region, traditionally related to water availability. Its greatest enemy is *Garuda*, but, surprisingly, at a certain moment of Angkorean history, the two became closely united into a single mythological being (*106*). This symbiosis is probably related to the legend of Vishnu sleeping on Ananta, the *naga* of eternity, before awakening to ride on his mount *Garuda*. The combination is related in the *Bhagavad Purana* where snakes are considered symbolic of poison, death and the underworld, while birds are symbolic of birth, ambrosia and heaven.

The *naga* is the mythological animal which appears most frequently in Khmer art. Often it frames a pediment with heads at both ends or features on lintels over temple doors. As a long scaly snake it is also forming balustrades along the temple causeways, and at the edges of water basins such as Srah Srang (*104* and *108*). This balustrade function, in which both ends terminate in a large raised hood, often combined with *Garuda*, is unique to Khmer art, being unknown in India.

Some *naga*s enjoyed a particularly important role in Khmer mythology, like Vasuki, who offered himself for the Churning of the Ocean of Milk, and Ananta, who served as Vishnu's sleeping couch.

In Buddhist mythology, the king of the *naga*s, Muchalinda, saved and protected the Buddha from drowning; becoming thus a very powerful symbol. The image of Buddha sitting in meditation on the three coils of the *naga*, protected at the back and over his head by the seven-headed hood of Muchalinda, is one of the most venerated Buddhist icons of the Khmers, occurring frequently in stone and bronze sculpture from the 11th century onwards (see page 59).

102 Devata. *Wat Nokor.*

103 Kala *from a lintel at Muang Tam, north-east Thailand.*

108 *Opposite: The bald-headed* nagas *of Preah Vihear.* *(Photo: M. Freeman)*

104 Nagas *on the terrace of Preah Palilay.*

105 Makara *at the end of a lintel. Petchaburi Museum, Thailand.*
(Photo: M. Freeman)

106 Naga *and garuda combined, Srah Srang.*

107 Kala *from a lintel. Wat Nokor.*

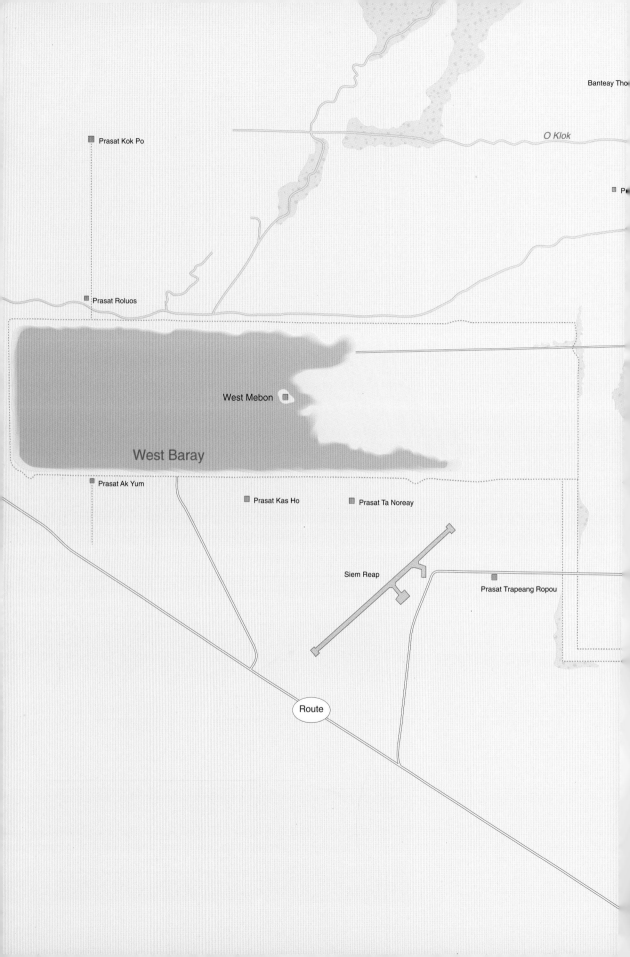

Banteay Tho

O Klok

Prasat Kok Po

P

Prasat Roluos

West Mebon

West Baray

Prasat Ak Yum

Prasat Kas Ho

Prasat Ta Noreay

Siem Reap

Prasat Trapeang Ropou

Route

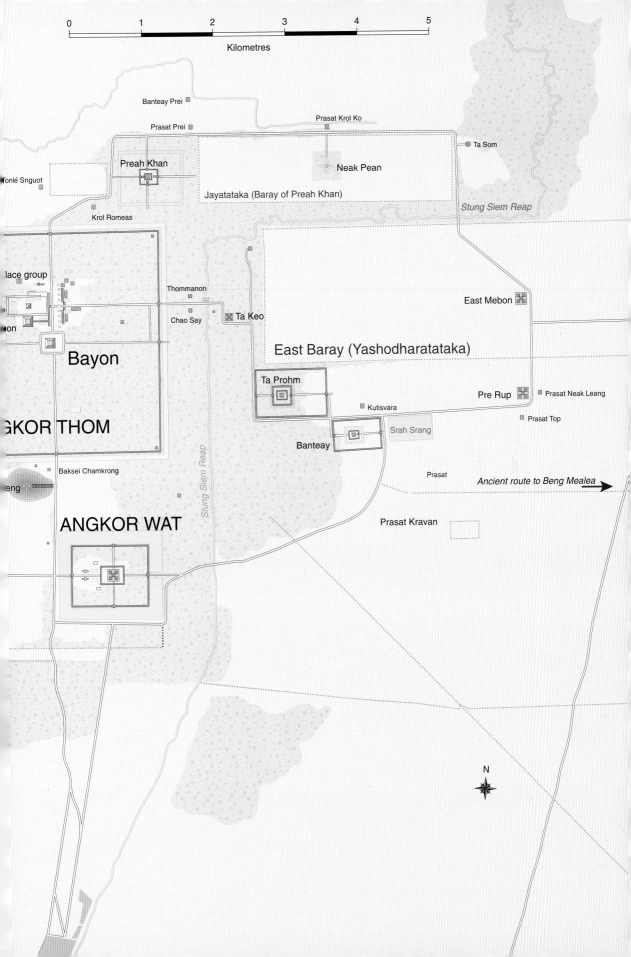

Kilometres

Banteay Prei

Prasat Prei

Prasat Krol Ko

Ta Som

Preah Khan

Neak Pean

Tonlé Snguot

Jayatataka (Baray of Preah Khan)

Stung Siem Reap

Krol Romeas

lace group

Thommanon

East Mebon

Chao Say

Ta Keo

East Baray (Yashodharatataka)

Bayon

Ta Prohm

Prasat Neak Leang

Pre Rup

on

GKOR THOM

Kutisvara

Prasat Top

Srah Srang

Banteay

Baksei Chamkrong

Prasat

Ancient route to Beng Mealea

eng

ANGKOR WAT

Prasat Kravan

Stung Siem Reap

N

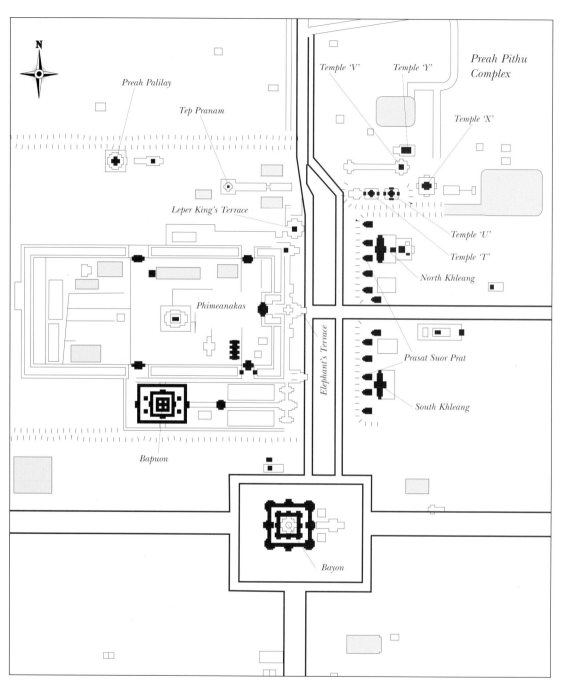

Preah Pithu
Complex

Temple 'V'   Temple 'Y'

Temple 'X'

Preah Palilay

Tep Pranam

Temple 'U'

Temple 'T'

Leper King's Terrace

North Khleang

Phimeanakas

Prasat Suor Prat

Elephant's Terrace

South Khleang

Bapuon

Bayon

110 *Map of Angkor Thom, showing the NW and NE areas close to the Bayon.*

Index of Locations

Myths and legends abound in the narrative reliefs of many Khmer temples. The principal sites are examined in the following chronological sequence:

Bakong
Banteay Srei
Bapuon
Phnom Chisor
Angkor Wat
Banteay Samre
Thommanon
Chau Say Tevoda
Bayon
Preah Khan
Ta Prohm
Banteay Chhmar
Terraces of Elephants & Leper king
Banteay Kdei
Ta Nei
Neak Pean
Preah Palilay
Preah Pithu (X)
Wat Nokor
Ta Prohm of Bati

The location and description of the reliefs presented here are based mainly on Glaize's descriptions (1944, re-edition 1993), supplemented by descriptions and interpretations taken from the research of French scholars, mostly from the EFEO, and my own extensive study of the reliefs.

From a general overview of the history of Khmer narrative reliefs, one can see that after the early examples at Sambor Prei Kuk, the tradition was neglected or temporarily abandoned, although small scenes with personages continued to appear, mainly on lintels. The carving of large narrative reliefs seem to have started with the building of the 9th century Bakong temple, and was fully developed by the time Banteay Srei was constructed in the 10th century. Here, the sculptors introduced scenes on the whole surface of the pediments in compositions whose sophistication has surprised historians, some of whom have sought the influence of Javanese art in explanation. In the 12th century, the narrative reliefs, known to us, consist of small panels, as, for example those of Bapuon. Then comes the sudden development of large-scale reliefs at Angkor Wat. While these may be viewed as continuous friezes from an architectural and decorative, point of view, in terms of their content and narrative they are eight separate panels, each one of which tells a different story.

In Khmer narrative reliefs, accessory figures – warriors, guardians, ascetics, attendant women and many others – form a significant part of the complementary elements to the major compositions. Animals, birds and trees are mainly introduced as decorative fillers, isolated from any narrative context; the popularity of birds is remarkable. Plants and vegetation are rendered in detail and some modern botanists have been able to recognise a good proportion of living species.

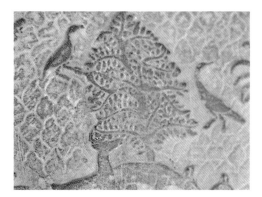

111 Birds were very popular in Khmer reliefs. Angkor Wat.

BAKONG

This Shivaite temple, built by King Indravarman 1 in 881, is located at Roluos, about 15 km southeast of Angkor. It is in the shape of a five-stepped pyramid; at the base, there is a small shrine with pediments which have the first representation of personages in Angkorean art (*113*). Traces of these figures, which would have covered the surface of the brick pediments, now largely empty, can still be seen. They are flying, or framed within palatial architectural motifs.

The most striking feature is the wall of the fifth tier of the pyramid (1.90 m high) which carries, on all four sides, a continuous frieze of reliefs with personages, framed by a finely carved moulding. It is the first realisation of this kind in Khmer art; unfortunately the reliefs are now in such a poor state of preservation that only four to five panels from the south face, are discernible. On the only undamaged one, it is possible to see a group of fighting *asuras*, sculpted in a style probably inspired by Javanese art (*114*).

112 Bakong temple.

113 Small shrine at the base of the step pyramid, N side.

114 The battle scene from the only well preserved relief.

BANTEAY SREI

The temple, originally belonging to the Ishvarapura complex, was named Banteay Srei (meaning citadel of women) in recent times. It is not located in the Angkor area, but 25 km northeast of Bayon. The quality of its carving is unusual, since it was not built by a king, but by his *guru* Yajnavaraha, and his younger brother Vishnukumara.

Initiated after the mid-10th century, during the reign of Rajendravarman, it was consecrated in 967 under the reign of Jayavarman V.

The Brahmin Yajnavaraha, of royal descent, was a person of exceptional calibre, who had a very important role in the education of the heir to the throne, the young 10-year-old prince who would become Jayavarman V. It seems that the boy was saved by his *guru* from the conspiracy which killed his father Rajendravarman (Jacques, 1988). For this reason, the prince resided in the house of his *guru*, as was customary among all disciples in India. Besides his complete familiarity with the various Hindu doctrines, Yajnavaraha knew about the nature of the elements, the source of knowledge, Buddhism, medicine, astronomy, music, and theatre. His younger brother was a grammarian who made copies of the Shivaite texts.

The main divinity to whom the temple was consecrated carries the explanatory name: the *linga* Tribhuvanamaheshvara, "The great (*maha*) Lord of Three Worlds". It was housed in the central shrine connected to the tallest tower, decorated at the four corners with high-relief sculptures of youthful *dvarapala* (guardians), kindly smiling boys, holding a lance in one hand and a lotus bud in the other (**115**); both are attributes of Shiva. These adolescent guardians, unique in Khmer art, are replaced by charming girls and *apsaras* in the secondary sanctuaries. To explain the sweetness and harmony of this temple, with its lacy pink sandstone, and the ephebic guardians, Groslier (in Riboud, 1993) has suggested that its creator "preferred the young monks to the heavenly dancers".

115 *One of the youthful* dvarapalas *of Banteay Srei.*

The central shrine, of T-shaped plan, is flanked by two 'libraries'. The complex is surrounded by three (or four) enclosure walls with *gopuras*, called Gopura I, II and III according to which enclosure they refer (see plan, page 84). One of the striking features of the temple is its reduced scale, almost half that of any other Khmer temple, particularly noticeable in the doors which are 1.30 m high, and the inner dimensions of the shrines, which are only from 1.60 to 2.00 m per side.

The pediments of the 'libraries' illustrate narrative stories on a very small scale, sculpted in very low relief. However, the pediments of the east and west *gopuras* are decorated with significantly larger images, sculpted in much higher relief. Some of the 'elongated galleries' of the second enclosure, which are not 'libraries', are also decorated with reliefs, as are the ones at the sides of the entrance causeway.

The purely ornamental decorations are omnipresent; they include elaborate vine and

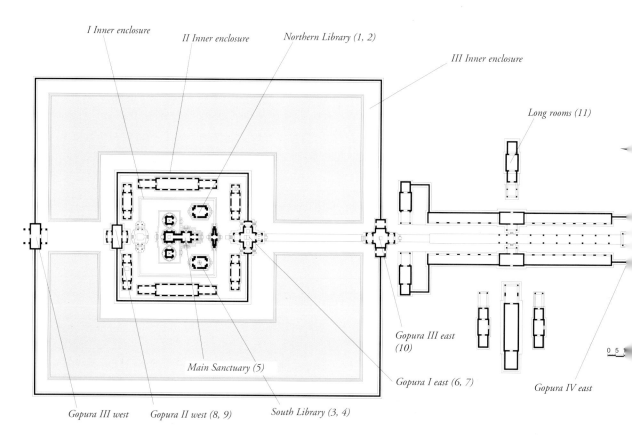

I Inner enclosure

II Inner enclosure

Northern Library (1, 2)

III Inner enclosure

Long rooms (11)

Gopura III east (10)

Main Sanctuary (5)

Gopura I east (6, 7)

Gopura IV east

Gopura III west

Gopura II west (8, 9)

South Library (3, 4)

0 5

117 *Detail of Indra from the pediment showing the Rain of Indra, S 'library'.*

116 *Above: Plan of Banteay Srei.*

118 *Krishna on his chariot, detail from relief of Krishna killing Kamsa. (Photo: M. Freeman)*

foliage scrolls, lotus flowers and mythological animals. The *makara* appears endlessly and ***Indra on his elephant*** is very common (***63***, page 53).

In the narrative reliefs, the sculptors have rigorously taken into account the space defined by the lobate shape of the pediment, accentuating the arrangement of the principal actors in the scenes, and thereby giving clarity to the work. The coherent structure is complemented by neat, tidy carving, verging on the meticulous, and an undeniable narrative verve (see the realistic representation of the storm and heavy shower). The subjects chosen for the four pediments are related to the divinities venerated in the two lateral sanctuaries. The Northern 'library', facing the Vishnu temple, has reliefs consecrated to the Krishna legend; the Southern 'library', corresponding to the Mahadeva temple, is illustrated with Shivaite scenes. They were initially interpreted by Goloubew (in Parmentier, Goloubew, and Finot, 1926), and later by other scholars. The results of their analysis are described below.

The numbers preceding the descriptions refer to the location on the plan.

1. Northern library, West pediment
The story of ***Krishna killing King Kamsa*** (***48***, page 45, details ***118*** and ***121***) is rarely illustrated in Khmer art, though it is also present at Angkor Wat on a pediment of the central tower. The scene takes place in a palace built of ornate posts or columns, of pyramidal design, with pointed superstructures like the ones of the stone temple towers. The decorative elements of the palace echo those of the temples, except in the absence of religious images, and give some idea of the masterly workmanship of Khmer wood-carvers in architecture made of perishable elements.

The two main actors, Krishna and his evil uncle Kamsa, are larger in size than the others, which emphasizes their importance and creates a perspective effect.

This episode is told extensively in the *Bhagavad Purana* and the *Harivamsha*.

2. Northern library, East pediment
The rain of Indra (***62***, page 53) The lower part of this tableau presents a pastoral scene with the young Krishna and his brother Balarama on their chariots, in a beautiful forest, surrounded by animals. Above them at the top, the storm is exploding, and ***Indra, on his elephant*** (***117***), holds the thunderbolt. Rather than a cataclysm, the artists represent a benevolent storm announcing the end of the hot season. The clouds are depicted as undulating lines, with the falling rain as parallel diagonal motifs, in which appears a *naga*, the symbol of water.

Although it is impossible to say exactly to which text this story refers, it seems likely to be that of Krishna and Balarama in the Vrindavana forest taken from the 65th chapter of the *Harivamsha*, dedicated to a lyrical description of the rainy season.

3. Southern library, West pediment
Shiva reducing Kama to ashes (***119***).
The composition of the Western pediment shows Shiva sculpted in his appearance as *Mahayogi* (the syllable *om* is inscribed under the hairdo), sitting in the *sukhasana* posture, and looking at Kama, the god of love, who is aiming an arrow of sugar at him, with the intention of annoying him during his meditation. Shiva gives his rosary to keep to his wife Uma, at his right; alternatively this gesture can be interpreted as Uma attempting to interrupt the meditative state of the god by presenting him with a rosary, to warn him of the imminent trickery. Kama fails in his intention, and is reduced to ashes by the ray emanating from Shiva's third eye.

On the steps of Mount Kailasa there is a crowd comprising the same people as those seen in the relief of Ravana shaking the mountain, except that here there are many more at the base, intermingling with the bull Nandi and tame deer.

The lower part of the relief shows Brahmins in a forest retreat, probably related to the story of *Bala Kanda* in the *Ramayana*, chapter 23.

4. Southern library, Eastern pediment

Ravana shaking Mt. Kailasa (*20*, page 35).

The composition of the Eastern pediment illustrates the story of Shiva enthroned on Mount Kailasa with his wife Uma; they both look at Ravana who is trying to raise the mountain by shaking it violently. The mountain is represented as a three-stepped pyramid, like Mount Meru, with a forest as background. At the base there are several animals (including lions, unknown to the Khmers in real life) fleeing in all directions, terrorised by the tremors.

On the second step of the pyramid, some supernatural beings with human bodies and animal heads appear to be in animated conversation, and one (larger than the others, to the left of the pediment) points his finger at Shiva; another, with a bird's head, seems to be complaining to Ravana. On the pyramid's third tier, there are ascetics with their wives; some seem to point at Ravana, while another looks and points towards Shiva, imploring him to intervene. At the top of the pyramid sits Shiva with his wife Uma, who, in fright, has snuggled up to him, in a gesture of amorous confidence. With the tip of his right foot, the god touches the mountain, to straighten it, thus avoiding a catastrophe.

Although the stories of the Southern library have been taken from Shiva legends, they do not seem to come from the same poetic texts. The composition of the Eastern pediment seems to be a faithful illustration of the episode taken from the 7th book of the *Ramayana*, the *Ravananugraha Murti*, while that of the Western pediment refers to a masterpiece of the Kalidasa version, the *Kumarasambhava*.

5. The central shrine

The three towers of the main shrine and the sanctuary, all united on a T-shaped raised base, are richly decorated. The doors and false doors are surmounted by lintels and small pediments decorated with figures. These represent gods such as Shiva on Nandi, **Brahma on Hamsa**, the sacred goose (*120*), Vishnu on *Garuda*, Nirrti or Yama on a buffalo, Skanda riding his peacock and **Indra**, usually on the three-headed elephant Airavata (*63*), repeated many times.

The most interesting representations are those showing the **Attempt by Viradha to abduct Sita** (central tower, western door lintel, *30*, page 37), the fight between **Sugriva and Valin** (central tower, northern door lintel, *122*), **Krishna splitting Kamsa in two** (northern tower, northern door lintel, *121*), **Krishna killing a demon** (northern tower, southern door lintel, *123*) and a curious **dancing girl** accompanied by two cymbal-players (northern side, central tower, *124*). Particularly interesting is a strange duo in combat which may represent Rama and the *rakshasa* Tataka, or, more likely, **Arjuna and Shiva** disguised as a *kirata* (*129*, page 91), since the boar who was the cause of the quarrel is represented below them. This animal may also symbolise the Brahman Yajnavaraha ('Sacrificial boar'), the founder of the temple.

6. Eastern Gopura I, West side

This is the only formal *gopura* of the first enclosure. Its reliefs are dedicated to Shiva. In fact on the Western side Uma (Shiva's spouse) known as **Durga** in her terrible aspect (*125*) is represented on the pediment, with eight arms, and fighting, with the help of a lion, against a demon ensnared in the coils of a snake; on the lintel, a **horse-headed god** holding two *rakshasas* by their heads is illustrated (*126*).

7. Eastern Gopura I, East side

A beautiful **dancing Shiva** (*127*) is carved on the pediment, easily visible as one approaches the temple from the main entrance. On the lintel, is a god grappling with an elephant and a lion.

8. Western Gopura II, East pediment

This is also decorated with reliefs of the story of the **fight of Valin and Sugriva**, taken from the *Ramayana* (*41*, page 39). Both of the monkey combatants are dressed and bejewelled like members of the Khmer royal family.

However, another story is told at the same time. In the right corner, one can see Rama just after releasing his arrow from the bow, with his brother Lakshmana crouched behind him, gesturing in the direction of the monkeys. In the

119 Shiva reducing Kama to ashes. (Photo: M. Freeman)

120 Brahma on hamsa.

121 Krishna splitting Kamsa in two.

122 The fight between Sugriva and Valin.

123 Krishna killing a demon.

left corner, the effect of Rama's lethal arrow is represented: Valin dying, with his wife piously supporting him, on his way to give some last advice to Sugriva.

9. Western Gopura II, West pediment

This pediment is not to be found *in situ*, since it has been transported to the National Museum of Phnom Penh (*73*, page 58). It depicts the ***duel between Bhima and Duryodhama*** during the battle of Kurukshetra, taken from the *Mahabharata*, and represents the culminating moment of the fight of the Pandava Bhima, when he jumps high in the air to strike the lethal blow at his enemy, the Kaurava Duryodhama. However, as Le Bonheur has noticed (1989), this scene could be interpreted the other way around: it is Duryodhama who jumps, but in vain, because Bhima, his feet steady on the ground, waits for him to land to release his final blow. This interpretation is better, because the more powerful one is, the less one needs to move!

To the right, the four Pandava brothers sit calmly and watching the fight, while, standing to the left, are Krishna with four arms, and Balarama holding the *phkak*, the typical Khmer long-handled club with two blades at an angle.

10. Eastern Gopura III, West pediment

This pediment is also not *in situ*, having been transported to the Musée Guimet (*67*, page 56). It tells the story of the ***apsara Tilottama***, created by the gods with the special task of ending the discord between the brothers Sunda and Upasunda, two evil *asuras* which were spreading desolation throughout the universe. The relief has 'frozen' the moment when the two brothers, each holding an arm of the *apsara*, argue over who should possess her.

11. Long-rooms

Several long-shaped rooms, mostly in ruins, can be seen at the side of the causeway. The pediments are decorated with ***Shiva and Uma on Nandi*** (first Southern long room, *128*), and with ***Vishnu***, in the shape of the *avatar* of the lion-god (Narasimha), tearing open with his claws the chest

of King Hirangakashipu (first Northern long room, *130*). On the ground close to the *gopura* III East, on the North side (Glaize, 1944), there was the pediment with the story of the ***abduction of Sita by Ravana***, the *rakshasa* king (*17*, page 28), with Rama and Lakshmana brandishing their swords.

124 A dancing girl is accompanied by two cymbals players.

125 Durga. Gopura West I, West side.

126 *A horse-headed god holding two* rakshasas *by the heads.*

127 *Shiva dancing.*

128 *Shiva and Uma on the bull Nandi.*

129 *A strange fight either between Arjuna and Shiva disguised as a* kirata, *or Rama and the* rakshasa Tataka.

130 *Vishnu tearing open with his claws the chest of King Hirangakashipu.*

131 *Dvarapala.*

BAPUON

This temple was built around 1060 by King Udayadityavarman II (r.1050-1066) at the centre of his capital city in the Angkor area, and dedicated to Shiva. The beauty of the architecture of the imposing three-stepped pyramid, its decorative elements including hundreds of relief panels, are comparable only to Angkor Wat. But it was also the most poorly constructed of all the Angkorean temples. It collapsed several times and was reconstructed on various occasions. It is now still under restoration by the French EFEO. Of its four enclosures, only the *gopuras* of the second enclosure are decorated with the famous narrative reliefs.

1. Eastern Gopura II, East face
To the south, a panel with *Ramayana* scenes: ***The Ordeal of Sita*** to prove her purity. One can see the young princess sitting on Rama's knee, then at the stake, raising her hands above her head (*38*, page 40) to implore the gods and Agni, the god of fire, to protect her from the flames and to be returned intact to her husband. Following this, Rama climbs onto the Pushpaka chariot and, followed by all his army, returns triumphantly to the kingdom of Ayodhya, to regain the throne after the death of his father. The Pushpaka is a magic chariot in the form of a palace, which, being pulled by sacred *hamsas*, can fly through the sky. Then follows a *Maheshvara* on his bull. In the upper part Rama and Sita are sitting on a throne.

An episode from the *Mahabharata* follows in another panel, the scene known as ***Arjuna's Penance***, concerning the dispute between Arjuna and Shiva, in which the latter appears as a *kirata* (hunter), about to to kill the boar, into which the *rakshasa* Muka had transformed (*61*, page 52).

To the north, another *Mahabharata* scene, the Battle of Kurukshetra, here focussing solely on the action of the main personages: above a group of musicians, the chief of the Pandavas goes to war against the Kauravas, then the duel of their chief Bishma and his death, in which he falls from his chariot pierced by many arrows. Note the bigger scale of the actors, which are larger than their horses, and Bishma, who is longer than the building in which he rests. At the side are other moments from the battle, and small scenes, one of which shows a man undressing a woman by loosening her sarong.

2. Eastern Gopura II, West face
To the north, a panel depicts the trapping of a wild elephant with the help of domesticated ones, then a series of carts and servants. A scene of ascetic life follows, with, to the left, an archer shooting an arrow at a woman. Nearby, a panel shows men wrestling, a monkey and an elephant.

To the south, below a man hunting a tiger, there is a duel over a woman, or a scene of beheading. To the right, are men grappling with animals, ascetics in the forest, women and archers, and a king enthroned amongst women.

3. Southern Gopura II, South face
On the western side are panels with scenes of daily life, a tiger pursuing an ascetic who climbs up a tree, a hunter killing a bird with a blowpipe, bulls facing each other, a praying ascetic, and a woman playing with a baby.

Beside this there are three episodes of the ***Krishna Infancy Story*** from the *Bhagavad Purana*. When he was a little boy, Krishna was gifted with an enormous strength; while still in the cradle he strangled monsters sent to kill him by his uncle, King Kamsa, who had received a prediction that he would be dethroned and assassinated by a new-born nephew. Three panels relate the story:
1 King Kamsa, a latter-day Herod, ordered the massacre of all young boys, as can be seen in the panel. A person, in frenetic movement, holds a baby by his limbs before smashing him against the rock of a mountain, where other little corpses are waiting for him (*133*, bottom panel).

In the panel above, a man and wife sit asleep (*133*, middle); they reappear standing, at the left, holding a little boy in their arms. This was the exchange of children that saved Krishna's life.
2 Above this, ***Krishna splits in two the six-headed naga Kaliya*** (*47*, page *45*), between two stepped terraces surmounted by bulls. According to the

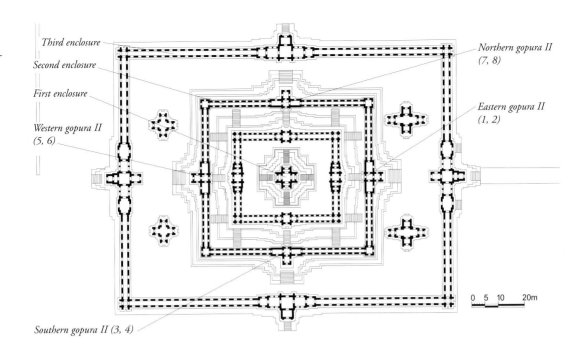

Third enclosure

Second enclosure

First enclosure

Western gopura II
(5, 6)

Northern gopura II
(7, 8)

Eastern gopura II
(1, 2)

0 5 10   20m

Southern gopura II (3, 4)

132 Plan of Bapuon.

Bhagavad Purana, young Krishna, wearing a three-pointed hat, holds the bull by its horns and throws it 18 feet away. However, since the animal keeps charging, the god brings him under control, makes it lie on the ground, and, holding it by the rear legs, twists its body.

3 Krishna killing King Kamsa. Another panel shows a renewed attempt by King Kamsa to kill his nephew by sending a mad elephant to charge at him. Krishna grabs it vigorously by the tail and catapults it far away. Finally, as expected, the wicked Kamsa is killed by the one he wanted to kill: we can see his torture: quartered, his body parted in two by the powerful fist of the god.

4. Southern Gopura II, North face

To the East and in the lower part, are panels with scenes of the life of ascetics; one seems to be churning the content of a jar, the other is suffering indigestion, while another one looks sick or dying.

Below, *Ramayana* scenes are represented: monkeys fighting giant *rakshasas*, the meeting of Hanuman and Sita in an acacia bush. Another panel narrates the life of Vishnu, twice represented with his usual attributes.

To the west, where the wall is truncated, there are panels showing forest scenes with ascetics, men, animals and intriguing fights.

133 Two episodes from Krishna's infancy. S Gopura II, S face. (Photo: EFEO)

5. Western Gopura II

This is the only *gopura* which is still in its original condition (1996), although precarious.

West face. To the north, panels illustrating epic fights and animals, then, below some musicians, a warrior on an elephant, preceded by an archer, and another warrior on his chariot passing through a cloud of arrows.

On the panels facing east, are a group of musicians, a *palace with ladies beautifying themselves* (*134*), a palace with possibly *Rama and Lakshmana* (*137*), and above them, a flying palace carried by *hamsas*, in which a god with three heads and four arms is enthroned. On the panels facing West, from the base, again musicians beating drums, a *fight on a chariot* (*135*), and a scene possibly related to the story of *Arjuna's penance*, in particular the episode of Arjuna receiving the magic weapons from Shiva (*61*, page 52), taken from the *Mahabharata*.

East face. Long panels with three narrative registers relate the story of *Kumbhakarna waking up* (*136*). In the episode of the *Attempt to awaken him* (*36*, page 39), the *rakshasa* is represented in deep sleep while the monkeys endeavour to wake him up by beating drums, hitting his head, prodding him with a stick, and by making a small elephant nudge him. Having woken up, *Kumbhakarna gets involved in fighting* (*37*, page 39) amongst a storm of monkeys sent against him by Lakshmana, which he eventually grabs by their limbs and catapults into the air or devours.

6. Western Gopura II, East face

To the north, a panel with mythological wrestling and fights, and an animal melee. In another panel to the south, the fight is between men and monkeys, with, at the centre, a dying figure on a very large scale, supported by a tiny elephant. Not far away, boars are fighting, an archer shoots an arrow at a monster with a human head, and two mythological horses face each other.

7. Northern Gopura II, North face

To the east, the panels with scenes of the *Ramayana*, show various elements of the Battle of Lanka.

The bottom panel shows *Rama on his chariot* pulled by three horses (*138*). The panel above shows the *fight of a monkey and a rakshasa* (*139*). Then follows Hanuman, the monkey general, who, having jumped on the *chariot of Ravana* with ten heads and a thousand arms, pulled by monsters with human heads, is about to disfigure him (*140*). Following this, *Ravana* appears standing erect on his chariot pulled by horses with human heads (*141*). He returns Rama's arrowshot, who is curiously balancing one foot on the head and the other on the tail of Hanuman, in the act of twisting the head of one of Ravana's horses.

The following panel shows *Hanuman giving the ring to Sita,* while she is a prisoner in Ravana's palace (*35*, page 39). The action takes place in a small acacia bush, where Hanuman manages to give Sita the ring that will prove the sincerity of his mission.

Above this, another panel shows *Ravana on his magic chariot* pulled by animals with human heads (*142*).

Along the first window of the gallery, there are animal decorative motifs.

To the West, besides decorative motifs of animals and small figures, is a panel once again showing the Battle of Lanka. One of Ravana's sons, Indrajit, shoots magic arrows at *Rama and Lakshmana*, which turn into snakes and coil up around them while the monkeys shriek (*143*, lower panel, page 96). Then Garuda lands from the sky, sets them free and cures them by touching their wounds (*143*, top panel).

Another panel shows the *Ramayana* story of Rama on the Pushpaka pulled by *hamsas* returning to Ayodhya after bidding farewell to the friendly monkeys. Nearby, below a panel with two elephants confronting each other and an ascetic churning something, there is the alliance between Rama and Lakshmana and Sugriva who, kneeling on the floor, laments his exile on Mount Malaya at the hands of his brother Valin. Then, a panel with the story of Rama killing Valin. This happens during the fight between the two brothers Sugriva and Valin, when Rama, in order

134 Palace ladies. W Gopura II, W face.

135 Fight on a chariot. W Gopura II, W face.

*137 A palace with possibly Rama and Lakshmana.
W Gopura II, W face.*

136 The story of Kumbhakarna. W Gopura II, E face.

*138 Rama on his chariot pulled by three horses.
N Gopura II, N face.*

to guarantee the victory of his ally Sugriva, ambushes Valin by fatally shooting him in the back with an arrow.

8. Northern Gopura, South face

To the east, bulls and horses facing each other, then again the *Ramayana* scene of the alliance of Rama and Sugriva in the presence of Lakshmana. To the West, scenes of combat between men and animals; in a corner, Sita in the acacia bush.

Probably coming from this *gopura* are the blocks lying on the ground, in the site area (1997): the Battle of Kurukshetra; Arjuna's chariot driven by Krishna?; **Hanuman receiving the ring from Sita**, while prisoner in Ravana's palace (**35**, page 39); Two elephants confronting each other; **Rama and Lakshmana consoling Sugriva** who, kneeling on the floor, cries after being exiled by his brother Valin (**32**, page 39)

141 Ravana erect on his chariot. N Gopura II, N face.

139 The fight of a monkey and a rakshasa. *N Gopura II, N face.*

142 Ravana on his magic chariot pulled by animals with human heads. N Gopura II, N face.

140 Hanuman, jumping on the chariot of Ravana. N Gopura II, N face.

143 Top panel: Garuda flies down to release Rama and Lakshmana. Below: Rama and Lakshmana are trapped by snakes. N Gopura II, N face. (Photo: EFEO)

PHNOM CHISOR

This temple is located at the top of the eponymous hill, on its eastern flank. It was built in the early 11th century, after 1018, during the reign of Suryavarman I, and at that time, it was called Suryaparvata, 'The mountain of Surya'. It was connected by road to Yashodharapura; later Jayavarman VII erected a rest-house at the same location.

It is accessible through a staircase at the base of which a causeway, facing east, crosses the entrance pavilions of the two enclosures before reaching a large *baray*. The group of monuments is composed of a main sanctuary tower, around which eight edifices are arranged in a courtyard surrounded by an enclosure wall, now in a dilapidated state. The central tower is dedicated to *Shivalinga*, and the north tower to Vishnu.

This little-known temple has been described by Lunet de La Jonquière in 1902-11, by Groslier in 1921, and by Dagens in 1968.

The iconography is scanty, due to the use of bricks, but there are a few pediments and lintels, some unfinished or ruined. The topics are either isolated divinities, such as Vishnu, Shiva, Indra, Kubera on the shoulders of *rakshasas*, etc., or legendary scenes, such as the dance of Shiva (a popular theme at that time), *Vishnu Trivikrama* (The Three Steps of Vishnu), Rama's birth, The Churning of the Ocean of Milk, Krishna fighting a lion and an elephant, and possibly the birth of Brahma. Amongst the most easily observable sculptural reliefs are:

Pediment with a **dancing Shiva**, over a lintel with Indra on his three-headed elephant (**144**).

Half-pediment with **Vishnu resting on the naga Ananta** with three heads. The half on the ground shows his spouse holding his feet (**145**). Below the pediment, is a lintel with a god over a *makara*. Another pediment shows Shiva and Uma riding Nandi, above a lintel with a divinity on a *makara*.

143a Looking east, with Phnom Chisor in the foreground.

144 *Pediment with a dancing Shiva, over a lintel with Indra mounted on his tree-headed elephant.*

145 *Half pediment showing Vishnu's wife holding his feet.*

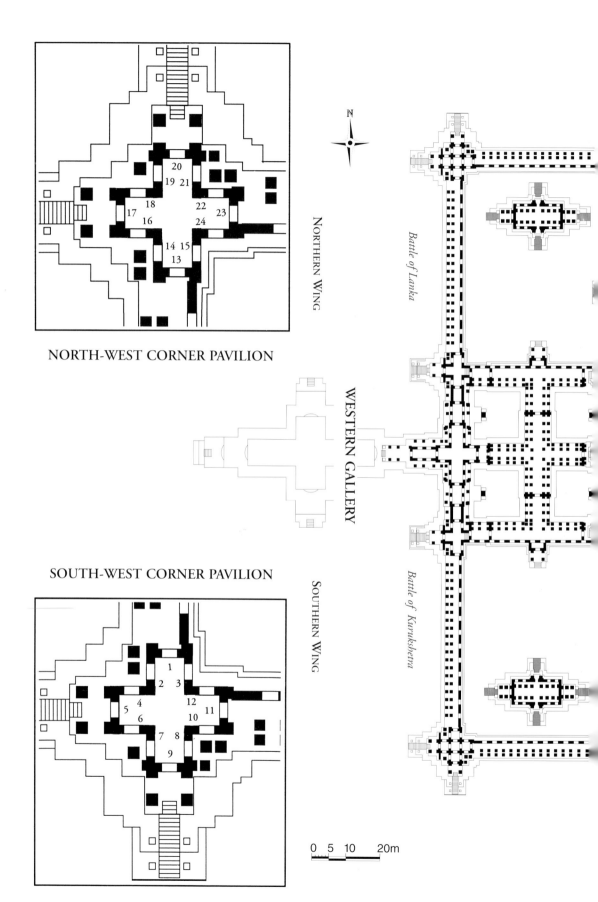

NORTH-WEST CORNER PAVILION

NORTHERN WING

WESTERN GALLERY

SOUTH-WEST CORNER PAVILION

SOUTHERN WING

Battle of Lanka

Battle of Kurukshetra

0 5 10   20m

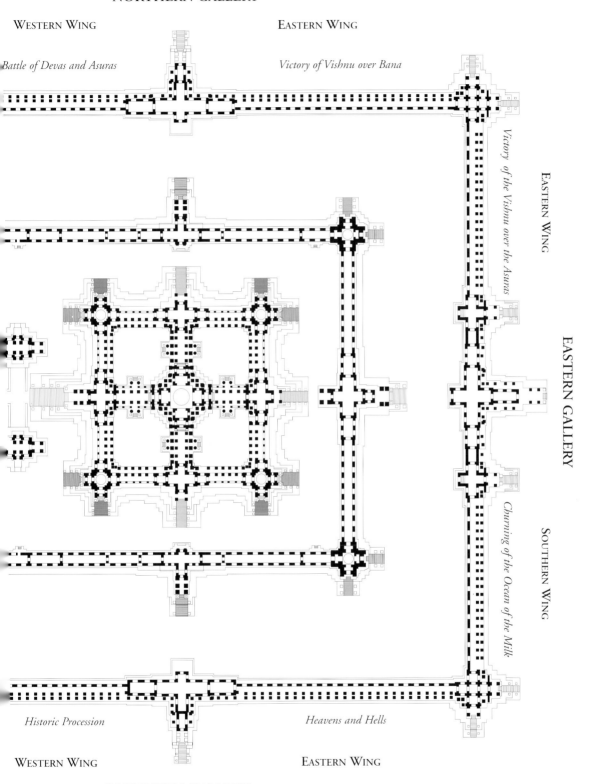

NORTHERN GALLERY

WESTERN WING

EASTERN WING

Battle of Devas and Asuras

Victory of Vishnu over Bana

EASTERN WING

Victory of the Vishnu over the Asuras

EASTERN GALLERY

SOUTHERN WING

Churning of the Ocean of the Milk

Historic Procession

Heavens and Hells

WESTERN WING

EASTERN WING

SOUTHERN GALLERY

146 Plan of Angkor Wat. Corner pavilions enlarged.

147 *View of the main entrance.*

ANGKOR WAT

This temple was built during the first half of the
12th century by King Suryavarman II (r 1113-
1150) in the Southeast quadrant of the old
Angkor city of Suryavarman I. It was dedicated to
Vishnu, and perhaps because it was also a
funerary temple, the main door opens to the
West (*147*). It has four enclosure galleries, the
third of which, together with the two Western
corner pavilions, are decorated with the famous
narrative reliefs.

It is the most magnificent example of Khmer
classical architecture and the largest religious
monument in the world. It was constructed, as a
matter of practical necessity, from the central
sanctuary outward and downward, and perhaps
the western entrances received early attention.
The carving of the relief panels of the galleries of
the third enclosure was probably begun near the

end of the king's reign, possibly as late as 1140,
and some reliefs were left unfinished in various
details; others were not even started. In fact, the
reliefs of the north-eastern quadrant were
completed in the 16th century, probably on the
basis of pre-existing sketches. They lack the
creativity of their earlier counterparts, and are
crudely carved. The larger figures, particularly
those of Vishnu on Garuda, were better sculpted
than the smaller, which were more summarily
executed as 'fillers' for the blank spaces.

The Galleries
1. Western gallery, South wing
The Battle of Kurukshetra (single 50 m panel)
The decisive confrontation takes place in the
plain of the Kuruk. Amongst the Pandavas,
Arjuna is the most worthy of royalty. His war
chariot is driven by Krishna, his closest friend.
The sculptors of this panel divided the event into

two halves: on one side, coming from the left, are the ***Kauravas*** (***148***, ***149***), and on the other, coming from the right, the ***Pandava warriors*** (***150***, pages 102-03). The contact point is in the middle, when the battle takes place. Here, as in other panels, the scene is the furious melee of two armies marching one against the other and starting the battle. However, unlike the other reliefs, there is nothing supernatural, no fantastic human or animal figures. The two armies of warriors, equipped in a similar way, closely resemble the Khmer army on the panel of the 'Historic procession'. Their chiefs, mounted on chariots or elephants, have the conical *mukuta* of the *devas* and legendary heroes. The soldiers march past in the lower register: some have breastplates and others carry a curved shield on their chests. A gong suspended on posts is carried by a group of soldiers, and beats out the rhythm of the march.

There is a large number of generals and one can see the typical posture given them by the sculptors, brandishing their bows in one hand and their arrows in the other, in a theatrical manner which repeats itself with a few variations all along the panel. Although this relief is somewhat confused, the details of the costumes, the headdresses, and armoury are indicated with great precision. The horses are treated in a half decorative, half realistic manner, and are shown in elegant postures.

At the base of the panels lie the dead and wounded; in the upper register one can see a fallen warrior, riddled with so many arrows that he cannot be laid down on a bed. It is ***Bishma*** (***72***, page 58), the general-in-chief of the Kaurava army, wounded by the innumerable arrows shot by Arjuna, in charge of a group of the Pandava army. Bishma, suspended in the air by the arrows penetrating his body, is in the process of leaving his will to his family; this is so long that it has taken 1000 years to complete.

The closer one gets to the centre of the panel, the more ***the melee becomes confused*** (***151***); it is an entanglement of arms and legs, but the stylised decorative attitude of the fighters, gives a solemn

148

149

148 and 149 Kauravas warriors. (Photo: J. Poncar)

150 Overleaf: Pandavas warriors. (Photo: J. Poncar)

and noble character to the battle. Some poses of the warriors are very acrobatic; the generals, when brandishing their bows, have their left arm quite unrealistically poised behind their heads, in order to see the person at whom they are aiming.

Towards the middle of the panel there are the interlocutors of the famous *dialogue of the Bhagavad Gita*: Arjuna, standing on his chariot, and Krishna, with four arms, acting as coachman (*71*, page 58). Proceeding towards the end of the panel to the right, the scenes become calmer, since considerable symmetry characterises the composition. It is the mirror image of the parade on the left, but depicts instead the Pandavas.

It is notable that all the characters and costumes are set in a recognisably Khmer world, and not an Indian one, as in the Indonesian reliefs of Borobudur (Fontein, 1990).

2. Southern gallery, West wing
Historic Procession (over 100 m long).

This relief deals with *King Suryavarman II*, whose posthumous name is Paramavishnuloka (*3*, page 11). In the upper register we can see the solemn audience granted by the king, seated on a richly decorated throne. He has a graceful natural pose, but not without nobility, and gives instructions to personages seated nearby. All around are advisers or religious people, and soldiers respectfully grouped. The rank of the king is demonstrated by the 14 parasols required by protocol, complementing the fly-whisks.

In recent times, the crowds of visitors to the temple have covered the image of the king with gold leaf, in an act of respect and veneration. In contrast, the demonic and hateful figures have been dirtied by the betel spittle of the visitors.

Amongst the group surrounding the king, one can see a *Brahmin priest*, recognisable by his high chignon (*152*). One of the main *state ministers* (*153*), whose rank is shown by his slightly larger size, sits in front, but turns his head towards the king, his right arm on his heart, a typical pose of loyalty and obedience.

In the lower registers there is a parade of the *queens, princesses and ladies of the court* (*154*).

The highest ranking ones are carried in hammocks or palanquins covered with a canopy ; attending them are the servants and slaves. They go through a forest inhabited by deer, and pick fruit from trees enlivened by many *birds* (*111*, page 81).

In the second part of the relief, the soldiers descend from the mountain and the infantry parades in marching order, escorting the generals and high dignitaries mounted on elephants.

There are 21 main figures in the procession: the king himself, and his *rajahota*, plus his 19 ministers whose names and titles are inscribed below them on the relief. Each has the appropriate number of parasols for his rank. The generals and dignitaries are standing on their elephants in poses full of nobility, their left foot on the war saddle, and their right on the croup of the animal; they carry a spear and hold a large leather shield for protection. The *mahout* who guides the animal, sits on his neck (*91*, page 67). The generals, like the infantry, have their lower body clothed in a *sampot*, whose long tails hang down from the belt to gather on the side. The *soldiers have helmets decorated with an animal head*, and carry round shields (*153*). The *horses* of some of the chiefs are sculpted in great detail (*155*). In many cases, *the king* (*156*) and the generals are conspicuously holding a *phkak*, the characteristic long-handled club. This instrument (never seen in use by ordinary people on the Bayon reliefs) is still used nowadays in Cambodia. It derives from Indonesia and is unknown in India. The parade continues, in a rather monotonous way. The soldiers at the end of the column are shown accelerating their march by lengthening their steps in order to catch up with those ahead who are marching in step.

In an evident attempt to introduce some diversion into the stereotyped poses, repeated many times, the sculptors have included some amusing details: the elephant of one of the generals, perhaps stung by an insect, suddenly turns his head in a menacing way towards the observer. Towards the three-quarter point of the panel, an interruption occurs in the military

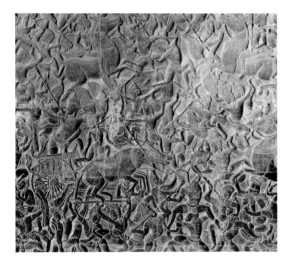

151   The centre of the battle. (Photo: J. Poncar)

152   Brahmanic priest amidst courtiers. (Photo: J. Poncar)

153   The King and ministers. (Photo: J. Poncar)

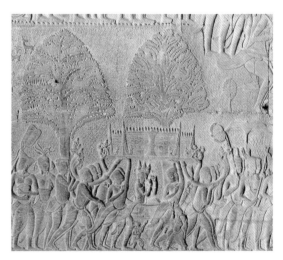

154   Queens, princesses and ladies of the court. (Photo: J. Poncar)

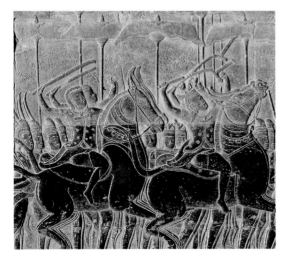

155   Horses of some chiefs, sculpted with great detail.

156   The king on his elephant holding a phkak.

parade, to give way to a cortege of priests:
Brahmins with high chignons, playing small bells.
The **Rajahota**, or royal priest, is carried on a
hammock (**157**), just like the abbot of a pagoda
nowadays. The ark follows, containing the sacred
fire, and escorting the army to sanctify the battle
and attract the attention of the gods. Numerous
porters are preceded by trumpeters, drummers,
conch players, and an enormous gong beaten with
a large mallet. In this group, there are also two
clowns dancing in a grotesque way and some
banner-carriers juggling with their insignia. The
same clowns accompany religious processions in
present-day Cambodia. At the end of the panel, a
group of unusual people appears, with
extravagant costumes, long vests with pendants,
bizarre hair styles with three or four plumes and
five rows of superimposed beads. The **general** is
covered with bracelets and necklaces, plus many
other decorative elements (**158**). The soldiers are
tattooed under the cheek and have an uncouth
physiognomy. Fortunately, an inscription solves
the enigma: "They are the Siamese", perhaps
incorporated into the Khmer army.

3. Southern gallery, East wing
The Heavens and Hells (c.60 m long).

The beginning of the relief shows three
different superimposed registers. Inscriptions
indicate that the upper two are leading people to
the heavens while the lower one leads to the hells.
In the upper two there is a procession of noble
people carried on palanquins by their slaves,
ladies (**159**) and *noblemen* (**160**), while the
commoners walk along quietly, some with their
children.

The people in the heavens live in the peace
and serenity of celestial palaces supported by
Atlases and Garudas (**161**), while in the sky
apsaras are dancing (**162**). The 19 men sheltered
in heaven may represent the 19 ministers seen in
the Historic procession.

Those condemned to hell are made to parade
before **Yama**, the god of time and death, who
brandishes clubs in his many arms, and is seated
on a buffalo (**65**, page 55). It is he who delivers

judgement, but it is **Dharmma** (in royal attire)
who pronounces the sentences, assisted by
Citragupta (**66**, see page 55), rewarding the good,
and punishing the bad by throwing them into
different hells which are at the base of the panel.
The reliefs present a *series of tortures* of refined
cruelty and unbelievable diversity (**68-70**, page 56
and **163**, **164**). Below are mentioned a few of the
32 tortures that the sculptors conjured up with
their sadistic and perverse imaginations.

Each torture is indicated by an inscription
revealing the sin of the victim. Crooks and thieves
have their tongues pulled out with tongs by the
demons who also put their feet into their own
mouths, and then throw them into a raging,
foetid river (since 12 different hells are reserved
for them, theft must have been very common!).

In the 'hell of weeping' those who are guilty
of injustice are chained, beaten, and slashed by
great two-edged swords; false witnesses are
skinned alive, suspended from trees and then
ground in a mortar. Those who have harmed
somebody, or taken the possessions of others are
plunged into a basin of molten lead and tin. In
the 'hell of the breaking of bones', the bones are
really broken by blows with a club. For those who
have destroyed the gardens, houses and ponds of
others, stakes are stuck in their throats. People
who have furtively seduced another's wife
(reference to love 'philtres'), or those who
approach spouses of second rank, are torn to
pieces by birds of prey and thrown into a lake of
liquid sticky pus. The women who indulge in
licentiousness are dragged by the hair and hurled
down a lake of marrow (meaning?); the
inscription explicitly indicates that this concerns
'women with flaccid hanging breasts', implying
thus that the punishment will reduce their
seductive power. State servants who abuse their
position to steal the goods of others, are thrown,
head first, into cauldrons. Those who cut down
trees where they should not, or those who defile
sacred places are sent into the 'forest of spiky
palm trees' (cactuses) where they have their neck
held tight in a vice; others are bound up upside
down in ropes. Those who steal flowers or

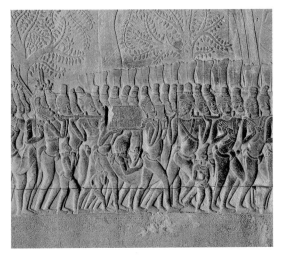

157 The Rajahota, *or royal priest, carried on a hammock.*
(Photo: J. Poncar)

*158 General from Síam, covered with bracelets and necklaces, and
many other decorative elements. (Photo: J. Poncar)*

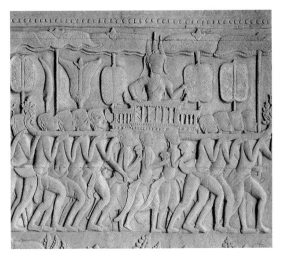

159 Ladies carried on palanquins by their slaves. (Photo: J. Poncar)

160 Noblemen carried by slaves. (Photo: J. Poncar)

161 Celestial palaces supported by Atlas and Garudas.
(Photo: J. Poncar)

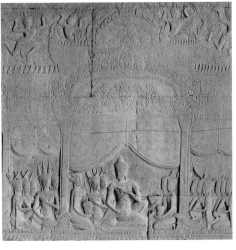

162 Apsaras dance in the sky over celestial palaces.
(Photo: J. Poncar)

disrespectfully pick flowers from sacred gardens, are tied to a tree, and demons hammer nails into their heads with great blows, or they are devoured by dogs or by birds of prey – a torture quite similar to that reserved for the 'great criminals'. Finally, the special torture reserved for thieves, that of the 'cold hell', where the damned are plunged into cold water and, shivering, keep their arms tight around the chest. All these descriptions certainly provide a colourful picture of life at the time of Suryavarman II.

4. Eastern gallery, South wing
The Churning of the Ocean of Milk (c.50 m).

The depiction of the creation myth is rendered in great detail and with great precision. The gods *(devas),* including Shiva, help Vishnu to confront Evil, represented by the *asuras,* in the effort to churn the ocean of milk, to produce the elixir of immortality *(amrita),* and create order out of chaos. *Vishnu,* at the centre of the panel (his figure unfinished) (*64*, page 55), stands on Mount Mandara that serves as the central pivot, supported by the turtle (Vishnu's second *avatar 4,* page 17). He controls the churning operation by the *devas* and *asuras,* who are pulling the great five-headed *naga Vasuki* (*165*, page 110), who acts as the rope around the churn.

The small figure flying above Vishnu represents (according to the *Bhagavad Purana*) another of Vishnu's manifestations. However, the possibility that it might be the god Indra cannot be ruled out, particularly if one considers that the two unfinished figurines over Vishnu's discus may represent the elephant Airavata and the horse Uccaishvara, both symbols of Indra.

The top (third) register contains a myriad of graciously flying *apsaras*, while the bottom register is full of creatures of the ocean; those closest to the churning vortex, are cut to pieces. To the right and the left of the lively scene of the churning there are the reserve armies, respectively of the *devas* and of the *asuras*. They stand, fixed in contemplation of the churning, ready to participate when required. One *asura* turns his head towards a neighbour to converse,

while another, with his leader, closer to the churning scene, points towards the gigantic head of the *naga*. The *deva* reservists are more disciplined, and nobody breaks rank. Behind them are horses pulling chariots, and elephants with war howdahs, and behind all these, a forest of banners and parasols.

Le Bonheur (1989) has noted certain incongruities in this representation: as Vishnu's lower left leg is bent over Mount Mandara, he should also be spinning with the churning motion, unless he is flying. Moreover, how could the land-based armies of the *devas* and *asuras* possibly reach Mount Mandara, planted in the middle of the Ocean of Milk? Moreover, the vase containing the *amrita,* the sole object of all this supernatural effort, is missing from the relief.

The influence of the *Ramayana* in the iconography of this primordial myth is indicated by the presence, on the side of the *devas*, of the monkey holding the tail of the *naga* snake, identified as Sugriva (rather than Hanuman), and, of a general with the headdress of an *asura*, identifiable perhaps as Vibhishana, Ravana's brother, and an ally of Rama. It may be that this character is in fact Rahu, who joined the action in stealth, hoping to drink the *amrita.* He was discovered, however, and his head was chopped from his body by Vishnu. In revenge, he regularly swallows the sun and the moon in eclipses.

Thus the Vishnuite myth of the Churning, here presents a novel influence from the *Ramayana*, also a Vishnuite text, glorifying the human and royal *avatar* of the god.

163 Hells scene. (Photo: J. Poncar)

164 Hells scene. (Photo: J. Poncar)

165 A multi-headed asura, possibly Vibhisaha, holds the head of the naga Vasuki. (Photo: M. Freeman)

166 Churning of the Ocean of Milk. (Photo: M. Freeman)

5. Eastern gallery, North wing

The Victory of Vishnu over the **asuras** (c.50 m).

This is the story of the battle of Vishnu, mounted – as usual – on Garuda, alone against hordes of *asuras*, attacking him from both sides. Some *asuras* are riding on large birds; their chariots pulled by dragons or mythical horses. Thanks to Garuda struggling with the elephants of the *asura* generals, and to Vishnu's courage, the god's victory is assured.

The quality of this relief, as well as of the following one on the victory of Vishnu over Bana, is notably inferior to that of the others examined so far. They were sculpted during the 16th century, probably copied by local and hired foreign artists from earlier designs, using stencils (Le Bonheur, 1995). According to 16th Khmer inscriptions, the work to complete these two reliefs, left unfinished in the 12th century, started under the rule of King Ang Chan, and probably ended during the reign of his son Paramaraja I, in 1563-64.

6. Northern gallery, East wing

Victory of Krishna over the **asura** *Bana* (c.60 m).

This story is taken from the *Harivamsha* text. It concerns the adventures of Aniruddha when he was captured and made prisoner by the *asura* Bana, after the latter heard that he wanted to marry his daughter. On learning this, Krishna, together with Balarama and Pradyumna, hastened immediately to the city of Shonitapura to rescue Aniruddha. Before entering the city, with the help of Garuda he extinguished the legendary 'five fires', and then annihilated the army of the *asuras*, in a battle culminating with the beheading of Bana.

In the relief, the scene starts with *Garuda, carrying Vishnu on his shoulders* (*54*, page 47), appearing in the middle of a great army of *devas* recognisable by their conical *mukuta*, marching in battle order, led by musicians. Vishnu is represented here with eight arms, brandishing the traditional attributes: arrow, javelin, discus, conch, club, thunderbolt, bow and shield. It is impossible to count his faces; the texts say they

number 1,000. He is accompanied by two heroes on the wings of Garuda, one being his brother Balarama and the other possibly his son Pradyumna.

When they arrive in front of the city where the enemy is ready to do battle, the three heroes are stopped by a wall of fire. However, according to the text, *Garuda* extinguishes it (*49*, page 45) with water taken from the Ganges that he transforms into rain. In fact, the relief only shows Garuda clearing the wall of flames. Once on the other side of the blaze, besides Garuda, is *Agni*, represented as a giant with six heads and four arms mounted on a rhinoceros (*52*, page 46), and preparing to fight. Krishna's army, advancing swiftly, enters the city and attacks Bana's soldiers, to annihilate them. A furious melee follows, with the combatants inextricably locked together. Krishna appears again on Garuda; this time the god only has four arms and fights with the bow, disc, and club. Then he reappears with a thousand faces and eight arms, accompanied by his acolytes. As he progresses he finds himself face-to-face with Bana, his chariot pulled by two mythical lions (looking rather grotesque).

The *asura* Bana whirls his thousand arms, but Krishna reduces them to two. When he is dealing Bana the final blow, Shiva intervenes to ask for mercy, having previously promised immortality to Bana. Eventually, after much fighting, Krishna, by the power of his sacred and magic weapons, manages to win the battle.

The conclusion of the story is represented at the right extremity of the panel. Shiva can be seen, depicted in Chinese aspect, on a high pedestal (probably symbolic of a mountain) receiving the respects of *Krishna*, with a thousand heads (**167**). He had won the battle against Bana, and kneels before Shiva, on a lower pedestal, his hands joined on his chest. In between the two, on the lowest pedestal, are Ganesha and Parvati, Krishna's wife (or maybe Skanda); ascetics and bird-maidens *(kinnari)* fill the flanks of the mountain.

Shiva (*168*), as mentioned above, is not depicted in a Khmer manner but in a Chinese

167 Krishna paying respect to Shiva.

168 Shiva.

169 Clouds scattered over the battlefield treated in a Chinese manner.

170 Fire, as illustrated by the Chinese artisans who assisted in the completion this relief in the 16th century.

style, with an oval face with long thin beard, covered by scarves and jewellery, and with several ribbons around his hairdo (bizarre for an ascetic). He does not hold the typical discus *(cakra)* but a sword, and is sitting on a throne decorated with hatched interlocking triangles, rare in Cambodia but common in China. The ***clouds*** floating over the battlefield are also treated in a Chinese manner (***169***), as are the ***flames*** of the fire (***170***). It is known that Chinese artisans completed this relief in the 16th century.

7. Northern gallery, West wing
***The battle between the* Devas *and the* Asuras** (over 100 m long).

This is a representation of the cosmic battle between the gods and the demons, the *asuras*, which had to occur in order to restore righteousness and order in the universe.

All the great gods of the Hindu pantheon are in procession, with their classic attributes, and riding their traditional mounts. There are 21 gods including Shiva, Brahma, Skanda, Surya, and the *ashtadikpalas*, (sentinels of the eight directions) with Indra, Varuna, Vayu, Yama and Kubera.

Each god is fighting an *asura* from whom he differs only by the shape of his helmet; this series of epic duels takes place in the middle of a confused melee involving all the personages. Note the realistic portrayal of some of the animals, as well as the emphatic pose of the generals.

Towards the centre of the panel, one can identify: Kubera, the god of wealth, on the shoulders of an *asura* with outstretched legs; Agni, the god of fire, on his chariot pulled by rhinoceroses; *Skanda* (*25*, page 35), the god of war, with six faces, on the shoulders of his peacock, whose legs keep the monsters harnessed to chariots at bay; *Indra* (*24*, page 35) on Airavata, his elephant, who holds an enemy in his four tusks. This sight and the noise of the bells make the lions rear up as a chariot is overturned. Vishnu occupies a prominent central position, opposing the terrible *asura* **Kalanemi** (*26*, page 37), with many heads (of which seven are visible), holding a bow while brandishing clubs and swords with his many arms.

Yama (*27*, page 37), the god of justice, follows on a chariot harnessed to buffaloes; *Shiva* (*28*, page 37) on a chariot pulled by bulls with two humps; *Brahma* (*23*, page 35) on his usual mount, the *hamsa*, holding the magic weapon *brahmastra; Surya* (*21*, page 35), the Sun god, on a chariot drawn by four horses; *Varuna* (*22*, page 35), the god of water, appears on a *naga* bridled like a horse. Finally, 10 not clearly identifiable gods follow.

The crises of the battle continue; one can see bodies distorted in agony. A five-headed *naga* entwined with the combatants spreads terror. Vishnu, on his intrepid Garuda, himself balanced on the bodies of two horses, dominates the scene and gives order to his soldiers. The *melee* continues (*171*) with warriors fighting in all manner of acrobatic positions, with individual combats multiplying in intensity; and the topmost register of the relief is furrowed by clouds of arrows. But at the end the *devas*, representing goodness and harmony, defeat the *asuras*, representing evil and disorder.

8. Western gallery, North wing
The Battle of Lanka (c.50 m long).

This somewhat confusing hand-to-hand battle scene, covering every inch of available space, is represented in great detail, with an animated multitude of beings fighting with incomparable rage and appropriate attitudes and expressions,.

According to Delaporte (1880), the poem of Valmiki, so often represented in India, has never been illustrated in a more powerful way. The monkeys do not ever suffer heavy casualties; they look overcome by fatigue, but, as the battle turns to their advantage, they resume their marvellous feats with renewed energy. Some are wounded by magic arrows; others, who have used the right spell to deprive the magic arrows of their power, stand up again and resume their fighting position. But a few, struck by feathered arrows, are lying dead on the ground. Warriors pause to recite the incantations which will render their weapons more lethal. The foot soldiers of the giant's army carry sabres with chiselled hilts, spears, javelins and clubs, and some are protected by shields. The monkeys carry only stones or branches, or more often no weapons at all; they bite their enemies wherever they can and arm themselves with the weapons they remove from the wounded or the dead. With their paws and teeth, they tear apart the fabric of the flags and parasols which decorate the chariots of the enemy kings and generals, pulled by fantastic animals. The way the sculptors render the bodies of the monkeys is the only attempt to define muscles in Angkorean sculpture; Showing the monkey's muscles in circles to emphasise their strength, they also portray the swelling of biceps, forearms, thighs and calves in a way which is closer to that of humans than of monkeys covered in fur.

A general view of the relief is impossible. One can only marvel at the virtuosity and imagination of the sculptors who managed to vary the details of the episodes, and the postures of the fighters so as to avoid any monotony or repetition. The melee is so dense that the combatants are completely entangled with each other. The

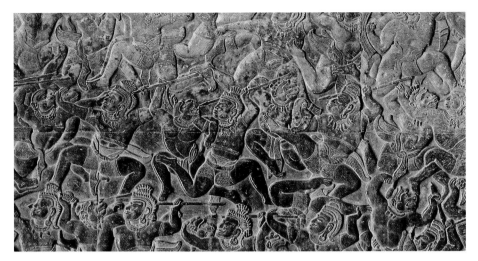

swarming animation and intense frenzy of this scene gives great vitality to the relief. The comical and the ferocious mingle to such a point that the viewer can no longer tell if he, or she, is seeing clowns or incensed warriors. They face each other, kill each other, dismember each other, poke out eyes, all with comical contortions and with a look of alarm on their faces.

At the centre of the panel, are the protagonists of the drama: **Rama balancing on Hanuman's shoulders,** in the middle of a shower of arrows (*173*, page 116). Behind him is his brother Lakshmana, while the renegade prince Vibhishana is recognisable by his plumed helmet. They stand in simple noble poses, in contrast to the surrounding excitement. Not far from them is **Ravana** (*172*, page 116) with his ten heads and twenty arms, standing firmly on his beautifully decorated chariot, pulled by monsters with unusual profiles. Between the two adversaries there is an admirably composed scene: the monkey **Nila,** standing on two monsters seen frontally, grabs and puts on his shoulders the body of the **giant rakshasa Prahasta** (*182*, page 119), at the same time as another monkey attacks the giant from below. Next to this, an **elephant** carrying the *rakshasa* Mohodara is toppled by a monkey, and his head – surmounted by a three pointed *mukuta* – expresses intense terror (*175*, page 117). Similarly, **Narantaka,** one of Ravana's

sons, is assaulted by the ferocious monkey Sangada who first slashes his horse (*176*, page 117). Next comes the turn of the sons of Kumbhakarna, firstly **Nikhumha** being attacked by Hanuman (*174,* page 116), and then **Kumba** by Sugriva (*178*, page 117). Elsewhere, a monkey, having grabbed a *rakshasha* by the arm, is about to inflict a **lethal blow with a stone** (*177*, page 117); others are striking the enemy **with thick branches** (*179*, page 117).

The battle becomes ever more frenzied, with the combatants assuming extreme acrobatic, interlocking, postures, and strange magic events take place before Ravana is finally defeated.

Sita is returned to Rama, but there is a complication: Rama refuses to take her back because she has been too long in the palace of Ravana and he suspects infidelity. "I have freed you" says Rama, but adds brutally: "but you cannot be mine again because Ravana has abused you". In reality, during the long time of her imprisonment, Ravana had never touched her. Sita protests her innocence, but Rama forces her to undergo the ordeal of fire at the stake.

In all these episodes the sculptors have followed the *Ramayana* story literally. Each scene can be identified and each personage designated by name. The action continues all along the panel's 50 m length, with a vigour and animation which never relent for a moment.

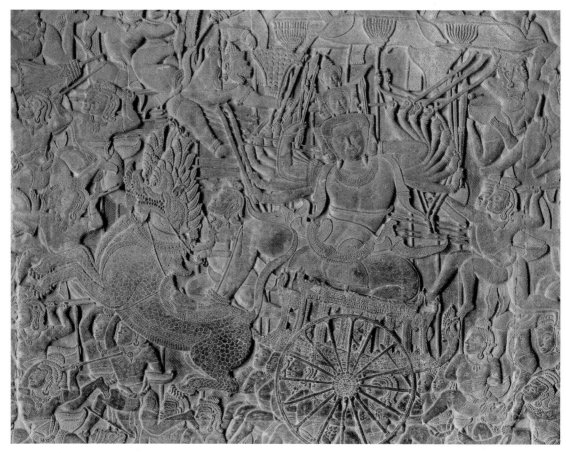

172 Ravana with ten heads and twenty arms, standing on his chariot pulled by monsters. (Photo: J. Poncar)

173 Rama balancing on Hanuman's shoulders, with his brother Lakshmana, and the renegade prince Vibhishana. (Photo: J. Poncar)

174 Nikhumha being aggressed by Hanuman.

175 The head of an elephant covered by a three pointed mukuta, *who was made to topple by a monkey.*

176 Narantaka, one of Ravana's sons, assaulted by the ferocious monkey Sangada. (Photo: J. Poncar)

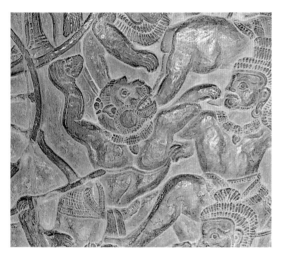

177 A monkey, grabbing a rakshasa *to inflict a lethal blow with a stone.*

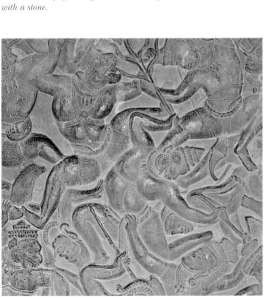

178 Kumba attacked by Sugriva. (Photo: J. Poncar)

179 Another monkey is hitting the enemy with a thick branch.

SOUTH-WEST CORNER PAVILION
The four arms of the pavilion's cruciform plan are carved with reliefs, in places poorly preserved because of water infiltration.

1. Over the Northern door A *Ramayana* scene is represented: ***Rama killing Marica***, the golden gazelle, which, by distracting Rama, would facilitate Sita's abduction by Ravana (*19*, page 31).

2. Northern arm, East wall A scene from the *Harivamsa* is sculpted here: Krishna lifting Mount Govardhana. Krishna, in the company of Balarama, is shown pushing up the mountain with his arm to protect the shepherds and their flocks from the torrential rain released by Indra's fury. Notice how groups of small lozenges are used to represent the rocks.

3. Northern arm, West wall A scene from the *Bhagavad Purana* showing the **Churning of the Ocean of Milk**. In the upper part, two discs representing the sun and the moon can be observed.

4. Western arm, North wall The story narrated on this wall was originally unidentified. Then Glaize in 1944 suggested it was a scene showing Ravana in the shape of a chameleon, sneaking into the apartments of Indra's women. Later it was considered to represent the story of ***Shiva Bhikshatanamurti*** (from the *Brahmanda Purana*), when the god appeared naked in the pine forest to test the self-control of the ascetics, stirred by jealousy of their wives (*181*). A further, entirely different interpretation could be that the scene refers to the argument between Shiva and Brahma about who was the real creator of the Universe, which induced Shiva to murder a Brahmin. To expiate this sin, he had to become a beggar for 12 years, naked, as in all other interpretations, without even a loincloth (*bhikshatanamurti*).

5. Over the Western door Representation of a scene probably from the *Harivamsa* when Krishna as a young boy drags a heavy stone mortar to which his stepmother Yashoda has attached him, ***uprooting two arjuna trees*** (*46*, page 45).

6. Western arm, South wall (over the window). The panel shows Ravana shaking Mount Kailasa where Shiva and Uma were enthroned. Ravana is represented here with many arms and heads.

Shiva is not shown making any move with his foot to make the mountain squash Ravana, as narrated in the Valmiki text, but is just sitting quietly in the Indian posture. The artists have represented the moment (Przyluski, 1921) when Yaksa, Vidyadhara and Siddha exhort Ravana to propitiate Shiva by prostrating himself and singing. Therefore Shiva is relaxed as he receives Ravana's homage, while the latter's hands are still fixed (motionless) to the mountain.

7. Southern arm, West wall (above the window). Here, the episode of ***Shiva reducing Kama to ashes*** is depicted. Shiva is shown in meditation at the top of a mountain, with Uma at his side, when he is the target of Kama, the god of love, who is shooting a sugarcane arrow at him. Shiva, furious at the disturbance, strikes the unfortunate Kama with a thunderbolt, whereupon he dies in the arms of his spouse Rati.

8. Over the Southern door The ***murder of ? Pralamba*** and the ***dousing of a fire by Krishna*** are illustrated (*180*).

9. Southern arm, East wall (over the window) Depiction of the *Ramayana* scene of ***Rama killing Valin***. In the upper part, the duel between the two enemy brothers, Valin and Sugriva, the monkey king. To assure the victory to his ally Sugriva, Rama intervenes by shooting a lethal arrow, treacherously hiding behind a bush, at Valin (*184*, page 120). Below, ***Valin lying dead in the arms of his spouse Tara*** (*183*, page 119-20), who has her hair arranged in a three-pointed *mukuta*. Below yet again, his ***monkeys are grieving*** (*185*, page 120). The panel close to the door, in several registers, shows the monkeys in a variety of attitudes and expressions. Przyluski (1921) has

180 *The murder of possibly Pralamba and Krishna dousing a fire. SW Corner Pavilion, over the Southern door. (Photo: EFEO)*

181 *Shiva Bhikshatanamurti. SW Corner Pavilion, W arm, N wall. (Photo: EFEO)*

182 *The fight between the monkey Nila, and the giant* rakshasa *Prahasta. (Photo: J. Poncar)*

184 *Rama killing Valin. SW Corner Pavilion, S arm, E wall (over the window). (Photo: EFEO)*

185 *Monkeys grieving. SW Corner Pavilion, S arm, E wall.*

183 *Valin lying dead in the arms of his spouse Tara. SW Corner Pavilion, S arm, E wall. (Photo: M. Freeman)*

pointed out that while Valin is represented with an arrow in his back, Rama is holding his bow (without an arrow) in one hand and a bundle of arrows in the other, possibly in the act of loading his bow. Thus Rama may not have been the one who killed Valin. Perhaps the sculptors departed from the original text in order to attenuate the impact of Rama's treachery.

10. Eastern arm, South wall
A poorly preserved and unidentified panel: at the centre a seated figure, perhaps Shiva meditating or teaching a group of ascetics.

11. Over the Eastern door
This panel is also not clearly identifiable, probably it represents Krishna (or Vishnu) receiving the offerings destined for Indra.

12. Eastern arm, North wall
Depiction of the Dvaravati water festival, where two boats with oarsmen (represented as superimposed) appear, with *apsaras* flying above them. In the upper boat are chess players, while the lower shows people playing with children; to the right a cockfight. An analogy with the modern Loy Kratong water festival of Thailand, has been suggested.

NORTH-WEST CORNER PAVILION
This cruciform pavilion is fully decorated like its counterpart at the SW corner. It includes some scenes that are particularly well preserved and of high quality.

13. Over the Southern door
The *Ramayana* scene represented here is Rama killing Kabandha, a *rakshasa* with an immense body, whose head is not on his broad shoulders but on his stomach.

14. Southern arm, West wall (over the window)
The scene sculpted is still unidentified, illustrating, in the upper part, a four-armed sitting Vishnu receiving homage from beautiful *apsaras* flocking towards him.

15. Southern arm, East wall
Again we have, from the *Ramayana*, the ***Svayamvara of Sita*** episode narrating the archery contest in which Rama had to compete in order to win Sita. At the court of King Janaka, flanked by an elegantly-dressed Sita, Rama, with a mighty effort, is seen shooting the arrow at the target, while below are aligned the ousted candidates (*29*, page 37).

Przyluski suggested (1921) that this relief may be related, instead, to Draupadi in which case the archer would be Arjuna. In the *Ramayana*, Rama lifts and bends the bow in a demonstration of strength, whilst in the *Mahabharata*, Arjuna aims it accurately at a target, in a trial of skill. In the relief one can see a target consisting of a bird transfixed on a wheel, perhaps identifiable with the 'aerial machine' of the *Mahabharata* (Adip.185,10), like a turning *yantra*. This would mean that the sculptors, rather than literally following the *Ramayana* of Valmiki, used some other text, or local tradition. Alternatively, they may even have confused the *Ramayana* sequence with that of the *Mahabharata*.

16. Western arm, South wall (over the window)
Illustrations of the *Ramayana* scene of Sita meeting Hanuman. Sita, while kept in captivity by Ravana, managed to arrange a secret meeting with Hanuman, in a small acacia bush. Next, the princess, attended by the kind *rakshini* Trijata, is seen presenting Hanuman with a ring as proof to Rama of the success of the mission. Below, there are several *rakshasas* in superimposed registers.

17. Over the Western door
Relief showing the *Ramayana* scene of Rama's alliance with Vibhishana. In the middle of a group of monkeys, Rama and Lakshmana are making an alliance with the *rakshasa* Vibhishana, who has been exiled by his brother Ravana.

18. Western arm, North wall (over the window).
Again a scene depicting Rama on the Pushpaka chariot. He is seen returning for his coronation to Ayodhya after his victory, on this magnificently

decorated chariot, pulled by *hamsas*, that had been previously stolen by Ravana from Kubera. A vertical panel shows some damaged figures of jubilant monkeys, some dancing, others blowing trumpets. According to the legend, Rama was accompanied by Vibhishana, Lakshmana, Sugriva and Sita.

19. Northern arm, West wall (above the window). The famous episode of the ordeal of Sita is represented here. The surface of the relief has been degraded by water infiltration to the point that the figure of Sita has completely disappeared. Sita was subjected to ordeal by fire soon after she was freed, in order to prove her purity. All that can now be seen, over several registers, is a group of monkeys humorously represented, the pyre, and traces of the figures of Rama, Lakshmana, Sugriva and Hanuman.

20. Over the Northern door

A *Ramayana* scene in which the giant ***Viradha attempts to abduct Sita*** in the forest, carrying her on his shoulders. Rama and Lakshmana attack him with flights of arrows (***186***).

21. Northern arm, East wall (over the window). Possibly Krishna is seated in a palace receiving homage and allegiance from a few seated men, in particular from a royal figure. The scene cannot be identified and it is all the more curious for what appears to be the bodies of two men stretched out under Krishna and his visitors (dead or drowned), probably referring to a local Khmer legend.

22. Eastern arm, North wall (over a window). More stories of Rama are sculpted in this arm, starting with the Introduction to the descent of Rama.

This episode was probably taken from the *Bhagavad Purana* "Introduction to the descent of Krishna" (Przyluski, 1921), but here relating to Rama, due to the great popularity of the *Ramayana* at that time. In fact, of the 12 reliefs in this pavilion, eight are scenes from the *Ramayana*.

186 *Viradha attempting to abduct Sita.*
NW corner pavilion, over the Northern door. (Photo: EFEO)

The event represented here has taken place before the birth of Rama, who also appears elsewhere in the same pavilion.

Vishnu is represented sleeping beneath a flight of *apsaras*, and lying on the *naga* Ananta, with his feet held by his spouse Lakshmi. In the register below, there is the parade of the nine living gods who wanted to beg him to become incarnate on earth (as Krishna). They are, from right to left: Ketu ('comet') on a lion, Agni on his rhinoceros, Yama, riding on his buffalo, Indra on his three-headed elephant, Kubera mounted on a horse, Skanda on a peacock, Varuna, riding on his *hamsa* and Nirrti on the shoulders of a *yaksha*. Below, on the wall flanking the window, are the moon (top) and the sun (bottom), represented as large discs behind chariots pulled by two horses, unusually represented frontally. The story should be read starting with the sun and the moon, and proceeding through the eight divinities, ending with Ketu, before reaching Vishnu, the destination of the caravan procession.

23. Over the Eastern door

The *Ramayana* scene of Rama's alliance with Sugriva, describing the meeting of Rama and his brother Lakshmana on Mount Malaya, with Sugriva, the monkeys' king, in order to plan an alliance.

24. Eastern arm, South wall
Krishna bringing back Mount Mahaparvata.
Krishna, mounted on Garuda (***187***), is carrying home the peak of Mount Meru (Mount Mahaparvata) recently captured from the demon Naraka. In this story, Indra pleads for help in subduing Naraka who has not only kidnapped almost all the beautiful spouses of the gods and the kings, but threatens to steal Indra's three-headed elephant, Airavata. Garuda is depicted together with his wife Satyabhama, and is followed by his army of servants carrying the remains of the defeated *asura* Naraka.

Le Bonheur (1989), has traced some representational sequences in the Krishna stories numbered here 5 and 11, the alliances concluded by Rama in the panels numbered 17 and 23, and in the panels relating the beginning and the end of the *Ramayana*, numbered 22 and 18.

According to Przylusky (1921) the episode of the death of Kabandha (number 13), and of Viradha (number 20), differ from the *Ramayana* story because in the text the two brothers (Rama and Lakshmana) killed the Viradha monster by cutting his arms off with swords, and not with bows and arrows as in the reliefs. Kabandha's death, on the other lintel, is shown to result from the two brothers hitting the monster with clubs, while at Prambanan (Indonesia) it is brought about with bows and arrows.

187 *Krishna bringing back Mt. Mahaparvata.*
NW corner pavilion. E arm, S wall. (Photo: EFEO)

PREAU CRUCIFORM

This hall (*preau*) on the west connects the gallery of the first enclosure with that of the second, providing a link between the first and second level of the pyramidal structure of the temple. Designed to gain more covered space, it is created by two galleries in a cruciform plan, raised over the surrounding courtyard, with four 'basins' between the arms of the galleries (due to the type of construction, when in use, the basins must have had a lot of seepage). The roof is supported by square pillars which are decorated, at the base, by reliefs of ascetics, now almost all badly corroded. Traces of the wooden ceilings have been found, sculpted with lotus motifs, with traces of painting and gilding.

At the extreme ends of the galleries there are four small oblong pediments with the following subjects: to the West, the Churning of the Ocean of Milk; to the North, Vishnu sleeping on Ananta; to the East, the battle between Vishnu and *asuras* (including Ravana); and, to the South, the first three steps of Vishnu.

COURTYARDS

The doors of shrines, libraries, and galleries facing the courtyards of the first and second level, all have pediments richly decorated with mythological motifs. Most of them are eroded by weathering, and difficult to interpret. Amongst the most interesting are:

First level courtyard, South central pediment

Lakshmana goes into a coma after Indrajit, Ravana's son, has used his magic arrows against him (*188*). Lakshmana was able to survive, but would have died if the monkey general Sushena (father of Tara, Valin's wife) had not administered a "sovereign remedy to Lakshmana's nostrils" and restored him to consciousness. (*Yuddha Kanda*, chapter 92). On the pediments, the monkeys are seen carrying pieces of rock from the mountain where the herbs of the remedy were growing.

Second level courtyard pediments

One of these pediments may recount the story of the **arrival of Kaundinya** (Bhandari, 1995), the first Indian prince, and the *naga* princess fighting him with an army of women, unique in Khmer art (*189*).

In another, a personnage who is possibly the king, with his feet supported by the paws of a lion with a *makara* head, and surrounded by parasol carriers, stands over three registers of worshippers.

Vishnu (or Shiva), with his consort, also appears in this courtyard, shown in a small temple, over three registers of worshippers (*190*).

188 Indrajit and Lakshmana. Pediment, first level courtyard.

189 Possibly the arrival of Kaundinya. Pediment, second level courtyard.

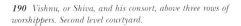

190 Vishnu, or Shiva, and his consort, above three rows of worshippers. Second level courtyard.

BANTEAY SAMRE

This is one of the most complete and well preserved of the Angkorean monuments, with decoration of exceptional quality. It was built in the mid-12th century, a little after Angkor Wat.

The temple consists of a central sanctuary connected to a long hall opening to the east, surrounded by a first enclosure gallery with four *gopuras*, standing in a courtyard, surrounded by the second enclosure also with four *gopuras*, the Eastern one remaining unfinished. On the eastern side of the courtyard there are two elegant 'libraries'.

The three complete *gopuras* have pediments with deeply carved narrative reliefs. They are larger than the ones inside the temple, of different technique and more beautifully modelled. Inside the temple, on the large pediments of the porches built on pillars, are reliefs inspired by the *Ramayana*, narrating episodes of the battle of Lanka, in which monkeys play a dominant role.

The pediments of the *gopuras* of the second and first enclosures (indicated here as Gopuras II and I respectively) are also richly decorated, as are those of the 'libraries'. The absence of *devatas* (*apsaras*) is probably due to the fact that the temple was never finished. Only a few of the pediments with narrative reliefs are described here.

1. Gopura II North, Northern face: the best preserved of the reliefs represents the fight of Rama against Ravana on war chariots, both sculpted in higher relief to make them stand out from the background of monkeys and *asuras*.

Southern face: a monkey stampede on the orders of **Rama mounted on Hanuman**, and of Lakshmana mounted on Angada (son of Valin) (**191**).

2. Gopura II South, Northern face: monkeys building a dam with rocks to allow them to reach and conquer the island of Lanka; on the half-pediment to the right, there is Vishnu killing an

191 Detail showing Rama on Hanuman from the southern pediment, Gopura II, N. (Photo: M. Freeman).

asura which he is holding by his hair, with rows of *kinnaras* (half human-half bird) and worshippers in the lower register.

Southern face: the monkey general Sushena brings Lakshmana the magic remedy to cure the terrible wounds received by Indrajit. Sushena (not Hanuman) is seen returning from the top of Mount Kailasa, on which the magical plants needed for the remedy were growing.

3. Gopura II West, Western face: the battle of monkeys and *rakshasas*.

Eastern face: Vishnu fighting two *asuras* who he is clutching by the hair; on the half-pediment to the right, a procession of gods, including Vishnu on a lion, Skanda on a peacock, Yama on a buffalo.

4. Gopura II East, Eastern face: over the secondary door facing south is the fight of

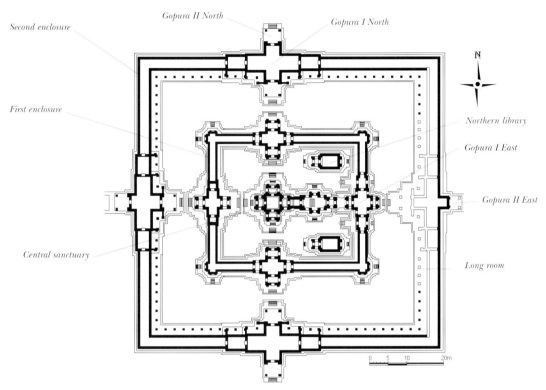

192 Plan.

Krishna against the *naga* Kaliya, and the ***Churning of the Ocean of Milk*** (*193*). The latter is on two registers with the shaft of the churn passing through both; in the top register, Brahma takes over the actions of Vishnu, the *devas* and *asuras* of the lower register, at the centre of which the turtle, Kurma, is prominent.

Over the **Northern entrance** is a relief with the Apotheosis of Vishnu, mounted on Garuda.

Western face: facing South, a pediment showing *Vishnu Trivikrama*, the Three Steps of Vishnu. Facing North: a nicely executed ***Krishna lifting mount Govardana*** (*53*, page 46) and Indra's sky attacking the *rakshasas*.

5. Gopura I North, **Southern face**: only the lower part of a pediment is readable. It represents two dancing *apsaras* with, to their left, some girls, one of whom ***plays the harp***; on the other side three girls making the gesture of respect, their hand on

their breast (*198*). Also depicted are ***Shiva and Uma*** on the Nandi bull (*195*).

6. Gopura I West, Eastern Face: the ***conjunction of the Sun and Moon***, represented as two human divinities, are each enclosed in a circle (*199*), surrounded by flying *apsaras* in the upper register of the pediment; the middle register consists of a row of kneeling ascetics, and the bottom register features a row of worshippers.
Western Face: a ***row of gods*** are shown on their mounts (*197*).

7. Central sanctuary The sanctuary tower is decorated with a series of pediments some of which show stories from the *Vessantara Jataka* (Glaize, 1993). The presence of Buddhist stories in a Vishnuite temple indicates the spirit of religious tolerance of the of the monument's founder.

On the pediment of the long room preceding the sanctuary appears **Skanda on a peacock**, surrounded by acolytes holding parasols; in the middle is a row of ascetics with raised arms, and below, the usual row of worshippers (**196**).

8. 'Librairies' The reliefs are not all in good condition and are of variable artistic qualtiy. One of the most striking is on the west face of the Northern 'library', showing the **birth of Brahma (194)**. Vishnu reclines comfortably on a corpulent Ananta (with a head similar to that of a dragon), and from his navel a lotus stem issues vertically to end in a flower blossom on which sits Brahma, surrounded by dancing *apsaras*.

193 *Churning of the Ocean of Milk.*
194 *The birth of Brahma, Northern Library. (Photo: M. Freeman).*

195 *Shiva and Uma on the bull Nandi.*

196 *Skanda on his peacock.*

197 *Gods on their mounts.*

198 *Musicians, harp players.*

199 *The conjunction of the Sun and Moon.*

THOMANNON & CHAU SAY TEVODA

These two small temples are intersected by the road of the 'Small circuit', with Thomannon lying to the north, and Chau Say Tevoda to the south. Both were built between the end of the 11th and first half of the 12th centuries, and belong to the Brahmanic cult.

Thomannon has generally poorly preserved pediments (described by Lan, 1972). Some are still readable, like the one over the South door of the long room, to the east of the sanctuary, narrating the **story of Ravana** (with many heads and arms) attempting to shake Mount Kailasa where Shiva is enthroned (**200**). The pediment over the door joining the shrine to the long room, depicts the death of Valin after the fight with Sugriva. In the northern wing of the Eastern *gopura* there is a pediment with Vishnu slaying two of his enemies that he holds by the hair, while the Western *gopura*, west pediment, has Vishnu on Garuda fighting the *asuras*. Another pediment seems to represent the reunion of **Rama with Sita**, shown holding hands, in the forest (**201**).

Chau Say Tevoda is in ruins and only a few narrative reliefs can be seen and interpreted.

The Eastern *gopura* has damaged pediments, two of which tell *Ramayana* stories: the one in the southern wing shows the fight between Sugriva and Valin, and the one in the northern wing, a scene with monkeys.

On the ground, there is another broken pediment with, in the upper register, a god (possibly Brahma) on a throne supported by *apsaras*; in the lower register **Tara holds the body of Valin**, surrounded by kneeling monkeys (**202**).

Also scattered around the temple are fragments of pediments depicting Shivaite and Vishnuite stories (including one with Shiva and Uma on the bull Nandi).

200 Ravana shaking Mount Kailasa where Shiva is enthroned.

201 The reunion of Rama with Sita, shown holding hands, in the forest.

202 Tara holding the body of Valin, surrounded by kneeling monkeys.

203 *The Bayon. (Photo: M. Freeman)*

BAYON

The building of this temple was started by King Jayavarman VII (reigned 1181-?1219) at the centre of his new capital city, surrounded by high walls with five monumental doors. In the central sanctuary a Buddha was installed, reflecting the king's devotion to Mahayana Buddhism, although Hindu gods were also venerated. The sculptural reliefs make little reference to a Buddhist world, and the many scenes illustrating everyday aspects of Khmer life show a preference for local values rather than universal ones.

The monument is characterised by the circular plan of the central shrine (*203*), and by the gigantic faces of the Bodhisattva Lokeshvara (about 200), which make it the most astonishing realisation of Khmer religious and cosmic symbolism (*205*).

Probably built over the foundations of an earlier temple, it was planned as a three-tiered temple-mountain with its entrance facing East. The gallery of the third enclosure, here called the outer gallery (140 by 160 m), is decorated with a continuous frieze of reliefs with historical motifs. The gallery of the second enclosure, here called the inner gallery (70 by 80 m), presents a series of narrative reliefs on religious and mythological themes. It is likely that the reliefs of the inner gallery were added later, possibly in the reign of Jayavarman VIII.

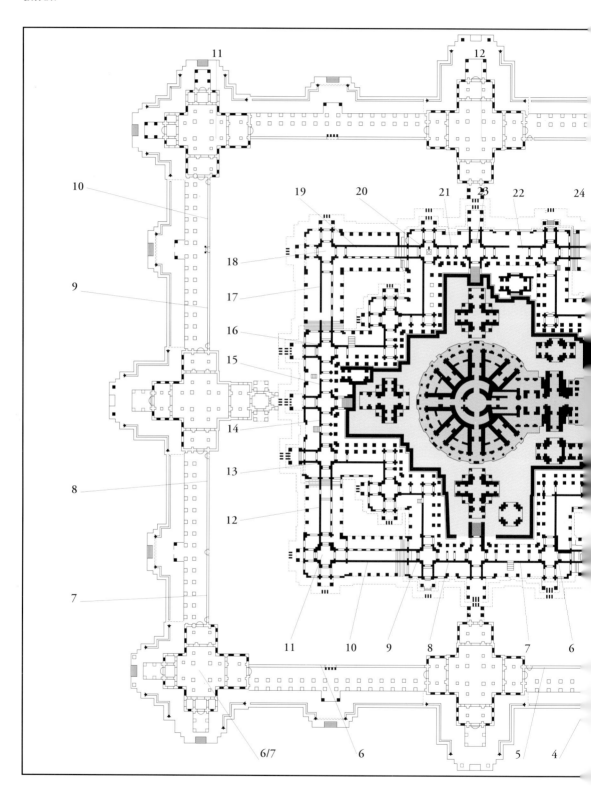

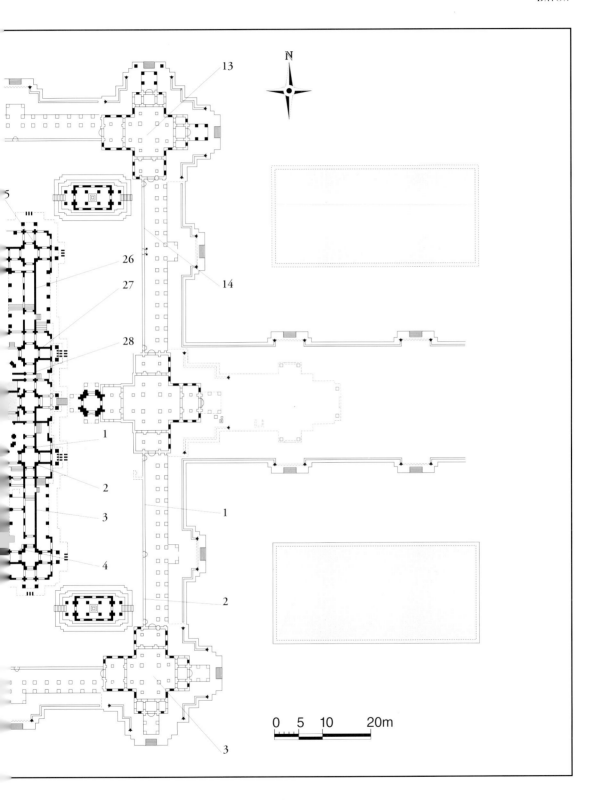

N

13

5

26

27

28

14

1

2

3

1

4

2

3

0 5 10   20m

OUTER GALLERY

Eastern Gallery, Southern wing

1. On three registers (of excellent quality), an army parade is depicted, going from south to north, against the background of a forest. The *soldiers*, armed with javelins and shields (*206*), are in the main shown with short hair and bare heads. However, a group in the register below have goatee beards, and hair unusually arranged at the top of the head. Some musicians accompany them, including a small one who jumps while beating an enormous drum with two sticks. They are flanked by cavaliers riding without saddle or stirrups, while the army chiefs, holding javelins and bows, surrounded by parasols and insignia, are seated on elephants guided by their mahouts brandishing their traditional goads. Towards the end of the procession the relief is brightened up by vignettes of *civilians* who accompanied the military (*97*, page 72); the supply services of the army roll past, including covered carts with lateral brakes similar to the ones still in use today. In the upper register, three princesses pass by in richly ornate *palanquins* (*207*) and, at the other end, is the ark with the sacred fire (similar to the one shown in the frieze of the 'Historic Procession' at Angkor Wat).

2. After passing through the gateway to the court, the *military parade* (*93*, pages 68-69) reverses its direction, and in the upper register, badly preserved, one can discern, with some difficulty, scenes of interiors and some ascetics. It is still the same type of parade, with the difference that the elephants are ridden only by their mahouts. The trees are sculpted in a realistic way, with *animals stealing coconuts* from a palm (*208*), while *monkeys play* in the branches of others (*98*, page 73). At the extreme left of the second register, one can see a buffalo attached to a tree, most likely destined for *sacrifice* (*209*).

Beyond this, four registers appear with scenes of interiors. The roofs of the houses, on which some birds perch, are apparently constructed with beams. The special type of hairstyle , the style of dress of the personages, and the objects hanging from the ceiling, all seem to indicate that the sculptor wanted to represent Chinese traders in animated discussion.

Southeastern Corner Pavilion

3. The carving in this area is unfinished. The first panel (facing East) clearly reveals the technique used by the Khmers in relief sculpture: starting from a wall which had presumably been prepared, they proceded to sculpt directly, first engraving the lines of the drawing, then gently carving away to create the volumes, before finally polishing up.

To the right, two charming *apsaras* dance. In the middle, people climb a staircase (under which there is a teapot) to join others sitting quietly, fanning themselves. There is also a group of ascetics and worshippers. To the left, three towers surmounted by tridents are outlined, the central one sheltering a *linga*.

Around the corner of the pavilion, nautical scenes are illustrated, with the *naga*-headed bows of the boats facing each other.

Southern Gallery, Eastern wing

4. This part, one of the better executed, narrates the *naval battles* of the last quarter of the 12th century between the Khmers (represented with short hair) and the Chams (wearing a sort of inverted lotus flower hat) (*94*, page 70). Two warship galleys with well-organised oarsmen and richly decorated prows appear to ram each other head on. Above, stand ranks of fighters armed with javelins, bows and shields. The corpses are thrown overboard, and often dragged away by crocodiles.

The king in his palace (*210*), shows the king, seated to the extreme right, in a larger scale than the others. He presides over the preparations and gives orders, while, below him, a gambolling figure resembles the clowns who still animate the rowing at the Water Festival in Phnom Penh.

205 Gigantic faces of Bayon's central sanctuary.

206 The army, and its accompanying musicians, processes against the background of a forest.

207 Princesses in richly ornate palanquins.

208 Animals stealing coconuts from a palm.

209 A buffalo attached to a tree, most likely destined for sacrifice.

210 The king in his palace.

135

211 A scene of everyday life, showing a woman and children. (Photo: M. Freeman)

Several species of fish are realistically represented (like the ones found today in the Great Lake) in between trees, either because of Khmer perspective or because the artist wished to depict the high water season.

The river edges, at the base of the register, depict, with a lot of wit and naiveté, all the small scenes of daily life; market scenes, *a woman and children* (*211*), *hunting* (*99*, page 74) or *attack by wild animals*. A woman delouses another person; another plays with her children; another cries over a sick person who is doubled up with pain; to the extreme left, a hunter is getting ready to string his crossbow, similar to a modern one.

5. Beyond the door, there is a panel of fishing with nets, using a junk possibly carrying Chinese with unusual hats, who seem to use strange devices for anchoring with pulleys. Meanwhile the occupants of another much flatter junk, are playing all sorts of games. At the base, are more scenes of daily life, including cockfighting.

Then, without any transition, there are palace scenes on five registers, each representing the floors of a palace: princesses dance surrounded by maids, or converse and play chess; below are gladiators and wrestlers, and a boar fight. Then a scene representing perhaps the king taking possession of his palace. According to the coronation tradition still practised in Cambodia, he would accomplish this by sleeping in the new palace; he can tentatively be identified in the reliefs as the large-scale reclining figure, who unfortunately remains barely sketched out.

The naval battle carries on: at the base, the Chams arrive on their warships and disembark, while above, the land battle takes place. The Khmer, shown as shaven-head giants, with crossed belts on their chests, clearly dominate. Peace returns, and the king, seated in his palace, celebrates the victory in the midst of his people, going about their professions: carpenters, blacksmiths, and cooks preparing a banquet.

To the extreme left, beyond the last door, a narrow panel, in three registers, shows people conversing below combat scenes.

Southern Gallery, Western wing

6. In this part of the southern gallery, only the bottom register has been completed. Here again there are *military parades* (*214*), where elephants play an important role and where war machines give precious information on Khmer armament. One is some sort of large crossbow carried on the back of the elephants and manoeuvred by two archers; the other is a catapult mounted on wheels. Some soldiers are descending from a hill.

The western corner probably shows the washing of the sacred elephants; the animals, protected by parasols, are brought to the river, indicated by a shoal of fish at the base of the register.

6/7. Corner Pavilion. Not decorated.

Western Gallery, Southern wing

7. Here, too, several areas have not been sculpted. In the lower register, a group of warriors and their chiefs mounted on elephants, progress through a forest and over a mountain (shown as small overlapping triangles clustered together), while towards the centre there is an ascetic sitting with his disciple, and below, another ascetic fleeing the attack of a tiger by climbing a tree.

High up in the second register occur some interesting scenes relating to the construction of temples: workers hauling a stone block on which a foreman is holding a stick (?), others carrying materials, and still more working at grinding blocks suspended from a special frame. Not far away, some sections of the reliefs give glimpses of the life of the ascetics.

8. Beyond the door, a long panel referred to by Cœdès as a civil war episode, represents a large movement of people in front of a row of houses, perhaps a street, with men and women gesticulating and menacing each other, while others *prepare to fight* (*213*). Above this, a kneeling figure to whom two severed heads are presented, seems to be in front of the others, and, above them all, another person in a palanquin approaches a prince who awaits in a palace.

212 Everyday life scene. (Photo: J. Poncar)

213 Scenes of civil war. (Photo: J. Poncar)

214 Military parade. (Photo: J. Poncar)

Nearby, there is a furious melee of people and almost naked warriors with the usual Khmer hairstyle, indistinguishable from each other, with several elephants involved in the action.

Western Gallery, Northern wing
Only the reliefs of the lower register are complete, those on the upper register being merely sketched.

9. Soldiers, armed only with sticks, seem to harass others who are protected by small round shields, preceded by elephants; they border a basin where an enormous *fish swallowing a small deer* can be seen (*215*). A short inscription helpfully tells us "the deer is his food". Another longer inscription engraved under a large shrimp, rather bizarrely states "the king pursues the defeated while fighting". In fact, this relief is incomplete as regards the upper portions, where the important personages would normally have been.

10. Beyond the door, another eroded inscription (the last), mentions that "following this, the king retired to the forest where he celebrated the saint Indrabhisaka". This parade through a forest, was believed by Cœdès, to represent the king going to a special retreat before celebrating the ceremony of Indra, according to an old Vedic tradition.

At the tail of the procession are women and children. As usual, the king, always larger in size than everyone else, is standing on an elephant, and, ahead of him, the ark with the sacred fire.

Northwest Corner pavilion
10/11. Very few sculptural reliefs are present in this small pavilion, and those that are are merely sketched.

Northern Gallery, Western wing
11. Only the lower part of the wall has been sculpted, though many parts are only sketched.

The first panel shows entertaining games in which athletes participate together with jugglers, tightrope walkers, and racehorses, as part of a public festival which is essential to Indrabhisaka's celebration. Above an indoor scene with the king, an unusual procession of animals gives an idea of Cambodian fauna. At the opposite extremity, a group of ascetics are sitting in the forest, while on the *borders of a winding river* (*216*), there is a group of women to whom presents are given, close to a large personage, whose sculpture is unfortunately incomplete.

After the door, there are more battle scenes, where the Chams reappear as the arch-enemies of the Khmers.

Northern Gallery, Eastern wing
12. The wall has almost entirely collapsed, apart from its two extremities, where one can find the frequent scene of Khmers and Chams in conflict. The Chams advance in serried ranks from the West, but this time it is the Khmers who are retreating to the mountains, seemingly without offering any opposition. The whole eastern part of the gallery is very animated and treated with great realism.

Northeastern Corner Pavilion
13. Parade of Khmer soldiers and elephants. In the centre of the pavilion there is a beautiful circular pedestal, like those usually reserved for Brahma statues; its style is quite different from that of Bayon, and it seems more likely to be of the 10th century, but its provenance is impossible to determine.

Eastern Gallery, Northern wing
14. In a grand deployment of armed forces, Chams and Khmers face each other again, clashing in the middle in a furious melee, where even the elephants take part in the action. One of them tries, with his curled trunk, to pull out the tusk of another which confronts it. Another elephant is shown in a rare pose, facing the viewer. Standards, insignia and parasols in countless numbers form a solid background.

215 A fish swallowing a small deer.

216 Representation of a river.

Notice, on the side of the Khmers, who seem to have the upper hand, the unusual, coarsely woven panels, meant to stop the arrows of the adversary without obstructing their vision.

INNER GALLERY

Our description continues by imagining that the monument is on our right when entering from the East. There is no longer a gallery in the true sense of the word with a continuous sequence of reliefs, but instead a series of independent buildings, cells and sections of galleries, clearly separated from each other. The various panels must be considered individually, as they only occasionally follow a common thread of narrative development in the subjects illustrated.

217 Shiva Bhikshatanamurti, in an ascetic yoga position.

Eastern Gallery, South wing

1. Room between two towers. On the wall facing South are reliefs showing ascetics, musicians, dancers, and animals in the forest, in a mountain landscape. **Shiva appears standing at a door** with his left arm held high (**217**). On the door lintel is a sort of lizard, a Khmer iconographic element still unexplained, which appears also at Angkor Wat, in the Southwest Corner pavilion (see No.4), and at Phnom Kbal Spean (Kpal Sban) in the Kulen mountains. This relief is better interpreted as a Shiva Bhikshatanamurti (page 50) rather than the metamorphosis of Ravana into a chameleon in order to sneak into the women's apartment of Indra's palace, as Glaize suggested (Glaize 1993). A similar scene is sculpted also in the Northern Gallery, Western wing.

To the left, Shiva is shown sitting in a small temple, and then, again, descending the mountain, together with an acolyte, to bless a worshipper. A cow in the act of suckling a calf is depicted in front of as rishi, on the mountain inhabited buy wild animals, including a boar.

In front and to the left, one can barely discern roughly sketched palace scenes, presided over by a royal personage.

2. Small room. In the upper register, to the right the relief shows the king in a palace surrounded by ascetics ; below this, are rural and hunting scenes; to the left (East face) stand Brahmins in front of a brazier near a temple over which *apsaras* are flying.

3. Low gallery. To the right of the door, there is an illustration of princesses in a palace amongst maidens. The large panel, on two registers, in front and to the left shows the often repeated military parade where the Khmers and the very likely the Chams mingle; a royal personage standing on an elephant, preceded by the ark with the sacred fire, is represented in narrative continuity over the corner of the wall, leading to the adjacent pavilion.

4. Southeast corner pavilion

The reliefs depict a group of marching warriors and a general standing on an elephant.

Southern Gallery, Eastern wing

5. Low gallery. This panel is dilapidated and difficult to interpret. It illustrates an army parade (of Chams?); a fight between two high-ranking personages; soldiers coming from the opposite direction, probably of the same nationality. Next follows a palace scene, then a man climbing up a coconut tree, followed by an enormous *Garuda in between the tail and the head of gigantic fish* (*218*), symbolic of the Ocean surrounding Mount Meru, here represented as a mountain inhabited by ascetics and animals. The illustration of the parade continues, with another high-ranking figure passing in front of palaces, either with empty rooms decorated only with scanty accessories, or with others occupied by princesses

smelling flowers or combing their hair in front of a mirror.

6. Small room. A large scale royal personage fighting against a lion (facing South) and an elephant (on the other wall, facing West) which he has brought down and whose rear legs he grasps.

7. Between two towers. Starting from the same wall, facing East, to the left, there is, above, a parade of soldiers, a king leaving his palace of which the main hall is almost empty, decorated only with some accessories (bow, quiver, and fly whisks), while a princess is seated between her maidens.

In front, from left to right, a combat scene can barely be seen close to another prince and his army, then a palace on the water's edge, with another building with some people standing around a brazier. The rock of the relief is exfoliating.

Following this, comes a procession of musicians and men carrying on their shoulders an empty throne, all coming out of a palace inhabited only by women, the lord being absent. In the lower register, the eroded relief shows a princess preparing to put a *baby into a cage* (*220*): giving the impression that the unfortunate child is about to be dropped into a nearby pond.

Next, a fisherman casting a net stands in a small boat, in the presence of a richly dressed *princess in a very decorated boat* (*219*) over which *apsaras* are flying. From the pond an enormous lotus-shaped pedestal emerges, for some idol or personage whose image has been obliterated, close to a group of worshippers who pay their homage.

It is possible that this scene serves as introduction to the legend represented in a panel to the rear right, which has been identified by Cœdès as the story of Pradyumna, son of Krishna and Rukmini. The boy is thrown into the sea by the demon Shambara, where he is swallowed by a *fish captured by fishermen* in their nets (*221*). In cutting open the fish, Pradyumna (who in reality is Kama, the god of love) is freed. A maiden of Shambara, named Mayavati (who is the incarnation of Rati, the wife of Kama), takes him

218 Garuda *and a gigantic fish.*

219 Pradyumna legend. A badly weathered relief in which a fisherman is throwing a net.

220 Left: Pradyumna legend. A princess gets ready to put a baby into a cage.

221 Below: Pradyumna legend. The boy swallowed by a fish is freed and offered later to Shambara.

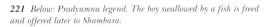

to a hiding place. He will subsequently marry her and finally kill Shambara. One can see the boy alive in the stomach of the fish that the king orders to be cut open, and then when he is presented to Mayavati who greets him with a wave of her arm.

Southern Gallery, Western wing
8. Between two towers. The panel facing West is damaged, although one can just discern a figure lying down in a palace, with his wife seated on a bed, lamenting.

Many Shivaite stories follow. In front, facing South, on a panel of very poor quality, the god Shiva is represented twice; standing on a throne, then on an open lotus, in the middle of his devotees, one of whom is lying flat on the floor; some sort of casket or reliquary is carried on a small cart. To the rear left, there is another image of Shiva holding the trident, over *apsaras* dancing to the accompaniment of an orchestra.
9. Small room. Facing West, at the base, one can see a palace, with some pigeons perched on the roof. Higher up is a view of a temple where a four-armed figure of Vishnu seems to descend towards a standing figure of Shiva holding a trident. On the wall facing South is a similar palace scene, with many closed, or false, doors, but without the four-armed figure.
10. Low gallery. Representations of flying *apsaras* and a standing person, probably Shiva, wearing a Brahmin's cord, receiving the homage of the Brahmins. Next, a mountain landscape with wild animals (a tiger devours a man) forms the background to a temple with two closed doors.

Some princesses are walking around a pond, while a group of three *apsaras* dance on lotuses; above Shiva is seated in his celestial palace, in the middle of his court.

Nearby there is the temple of Shiva, represented standing erect in the middle of a fish-filled pond, whose shores are crowded with ascetics and animals; a tiger pursues an ascetic, while other religious people are in conversation inside a palace and many devotees kneel in front of the god. At the centre of the panel there is a large figure, possibly the king, prostrated in *homage to the venerated statue of Vishnu* (*223*), which is standing, covered with real garments and ornaments, in a simple temple probably made of wood, surrounded by flying *apsaras*. This scene is similar to the one seen in the relief above.

Then follows a scene showing the organisation of a royal pilgrimage to the god's sanctuary. There are horses in the procession coming from a palace, illustrated to the left, with a staircase guarded by lions; higher up, someone seems to be giving orders, while many servants hastily get ready to depart. To the end of the panel, at the rear, are princesses walking around a garden on the shore of the pond, where one of them picks some lotuses.

Southwest Corner pavilion
**11. Incomplete reliefs of diffferent execution from the previous one, illustrating elephants and people.

Western Gallery, Southern wing
12. Low gallery. To the right, women appear in a palace whose main hall is empty. In front, Vishnu subjugating an army of *asuras* (according to Cœdès), is represented with four arms holding his usual attributes, standing on Garuda, and seeming to act either on his own behalf or that of a figure behind him. Next, a palace scene with empty rooms.
13. Small room. Another palace scene with *apsaras* dancing to the sound of an orchestra. To the left, facing South, women are swimming and picking lotuses in a pond on the shores of which there is an ascetic; above, dancers, and above them, a scene of two people vigorously wrestling.
14. Between two towers. To the right, facing North, illustration of a scene of the adoration of Vishnu with four arms, treated in a more complete way than in the reliefs of the outer gallery. Some coolies are hauling a stone block sliding on rollers, while others are actually laying the blocks with the help of a special system of leverage to put them in place; others transport materials.

222 A prince, or the king, prostrate before Shiva (see text page 148).

223 A figure, probably a king, lies prostrated, rendering homage to the statue of Vishnu.

Then, facing West, is the inauguration ceremony of the temple. This involves the adoration of Vishnu, whose statue is located over a gargoyle (*somasutra*) channelling water from the interior of the monument; flying *apsaras* and crowds of servants carrying dishes contribute to the scene.

A water festival scene follows (so badly eroded that the description is based on old records), with chess players on a small, richly decorated boat, surrounded by other boats, and a cockfight. (It is a similar subject to the water festival of Dvaravati in the Southwest corner pavilion of Angkor Wat). To the left, facing South, under a palace scene, are Shiva and Vishnu dancing, and several episodes from the lives of the ascetics; some meditate in caves, others swim in a pond among lotuses, not far from a bird which holds a fish in its beak.

Western Gallery, Northern wing
15. Between two towers. On the wall facing North are poorly-preserved palace scenes. Then, facing West, on three registers, is a parade of warriors, mainly cavalrymen, with two high dignitaries in their chariots pulled by horses. Facing South, the continuation of the parade.

16. Small room. Facing North, two lords of the palace are being entertained by young princesses as they are dressed by their maids; then, to the left, a temple containing a canopy on a step-pyramid, possibly a cremation pavilion. Facing West, an assembly of Brahmins, some of whom are around a sort of fire; in the top register, there is an archer stringing his bow, while another is getting hold of a bow.

17. Low Gallery. Another archery scene with, to the left, a lord in his palace.

The large panel has crumbled over most of its length. It represents the Churning of the Ocean of Milk, and what is left shows that it was well modelled. At the beginning there is an assembly of Brahmins, then under a flight of birds and *apsaras*, the body of the *naga* with the *asuras* towards its head, and the *devas*, helped by Hanuman, towards the tail. A replica of the *naga* crawls along the bottom of the sea, illustrated as a register full of fish. To the centre, the pivot is represented by a column resting on the customary turtle and held in place by the god in human form with four arms. Another figure tops the scene, as at Angkor Wat, above a capital shaped like a lotus.

The two discs of the sun and the moon are shown, as well as the ***jar destined to contain the amrita*** (***224***), the elixir of immortality desired by gods and demons. To the left, a god seated on a bird seems to want to pacify the group of *asuras* which complete the composition; their chief stands on a chariot pulled by fierce lions.

18. Northwest Corner pavilion

Only the inner corner-wall is preserved, carrying a representation of a military parade.

Northern Gallery, Western wing

19. Low gallery. Depiction of palace scenes on three registers, followed, on two, by a parade of servants who seem to carry offerings and are approaching, or following a larger figure; next, a mountain inhabited by wild animals (elephants, rhinoceros, *nagas* and other snakes, etc), with a pond and a sanctuary with closed doors. Below there is another, larger temple, which is also closed, its entrance guarded by *dvarapalas*.

Kneeling ascetics seem to welcome another sacred procession coming from the left, headed by two large figures carrying tridents. Perhaps they have landed on the shore because the scene becomes nautical, with a group of three junks, richly decorated and of large dimensions. The first two are surmounted by men with short hair and a lord holding a trident, the other by a figure wearing a hat shaped like a inverted flower, surrounding a central couple, engaged in a variety of amusements beneath a flock of birds. To the left of the panel, we return to the mainland, where, in a mountain palace amongst ascetics, several personages are enthroned; at least one of them is armed with a trident and may be Shiva.

20. Small room. Facing North, under a group of flying *apsaras*, there is a clumsily modelled Shiva with ten arms, dancing the *tandava* which regulates the rhythm of the universe. Vishnu is to his right, Brahma (with four heads) to his left, with Ganesha. Below this, a devouring Rahu can just be seen. On a part of the wall at the back, higher up the mountain, inhabited by ascetics, another aspect of the *Trimurti* is represented:

Shiva is seated between Vishnu and Brahma (***225***), looking down at an enormous charging boar.

21. Between two towers. Facing East, Shiva, seated, is shown surrounded by ascetics and women, of whom the first is his wife Uma; Nandi the bull is also close by.

In front, facing North, in a mountain landscape where ascetics are praying, Shiva appears standing at a door with his left arm held high. On the door lintel is the strange lizard of Khmer iconography, as seen in the Eastern Gallery (***217***), South wing. Glaize suggested (1993) that it may represent ***Shiva Bhikshatanamurti*** (see page 141), although the rather feminine look of the personage standing at the door may refer to the goddess Ganga (the river Ganges) descending to earth.

There follows the scene of Shiva killing Kama (also visible at Angkor Wat). The panel illustrates Kama, the god of love, shooting an arrow at Shiva in meditation on a high mountain, with Uma at his side; the god, furious at this outrage, strikes Kama, who is then seen lying on the ground with his wife Rati mourning him.

Next, the bull Nandi is represented on a hill. The panel ends with a scene of a prince sitting in his palace at the top of a mountain. To the left, facing West, a very clumsily carved Shiva and Uma on Nandi.

Northern Gallery, Eastern wing

22. Between two towers. To the right, facing East, a representation of ***Shiva riding Nandi***, with his wife Uma sitting on his thigh (***226***), passing in front of a palace where the *naga* king, with multiple snake heads, can be seen.

In front, (not visible in ***226***) the scene probably represents preparations for the cremation of a personage carried by the people visible in the lower register; above, a funerary urn and the cremation pavilion surmounted by a *kala* head.

224 *The Churning of the Ocean of Milk. Detail of the flask for the* amrita.

226 *Shiva and his consort on the bull Nandin.*

225 *Shiva seated between Vishnu and Brahma.*

Then follows (according to Cœdès) an episode of the *Mahabharata*, which we have already encountered elsewhere. This is the episode known as Arjuna's penance, dealing with the duel between Arjuna and Shiva disguised as a hunter over the boar that both claim to have killed first, and which is actually an incarnation of the *rakshasa* Muka. Shiva, eventually reveals himself and Arjuna submits to him. For this Shiva gives him the Pashuputa sword that will assist him in his future adventures.

To the left of the door is a seated figure in a palace at the top of a mountain, surrounded by women. Then follows the ever-popular legend of Ravana shaking Mt. Kailasa, but only showing Ravana, who has been almost completely squashed by Shiva under the mountain that he was shaking to annoy the god (The same story appears in a relief at Angkor Wat, where the sculptors have not forgotten to represent the Puspaka chariot pulled by *hamsas,* and at Banteay Srei).

On a panel at the end, facing West, there are two superimposed palace scenes.

23. Small room. Unspecified procession of common people, on three registers.

24. Low gallery. Several topics are represented here: servants carrying offerings (?), and, below a register of ascetics in meditation, a pond with stepped edges. Next, ***three sanctuary-towers (227)***, evoking the silhouette of Angkor Wat, surmounted by tridents, each sheltering a statue. The statue of the central shrine has been defaced, giving rise to two interpretations: either it was a Shiva or a *linga*, and therefore the statues in the other two sanctuaries were Vishnu and Lakshmi, or it was a defaced Buddha, and in this case, the two accompanying statues would have represented Avalokiteshvara and Tara. These three temples, in a natural setting of coconut trees, seem to be the objective of a pilgrimage of villagers bringing offerings. Far away, Shiva is blessing his devotees under a cloud of *apsaras*; it seems that there is a king, followed by his army, approaching to ask favours of his god.

The usual parade is depicted, with soldiers with shaven heads, musicians, elephants and horses; some princesses follow, carried on palanquins, as well as a large casket and a covered cart pulled by oxen. The procession passes in front of empty houses, then a king is shown stepping into his six-wheeled chariot at the exit of the palace, where some dancing is gladdening the evening of the departure.

25. Northeastern corner pavilion
Fragmentary elements of a procession on three registers.

Eastern Gallery, Northern wing
26. Low gallery. Here is shown a grand army parade, whose soldiers have two types of hair style: shaven heads and inverted flower hats. At the base the musicians are parading, the infantry with the cavalry, princely chariots pulled by horses, and others with a canopy pulled by men. Higher up, is the ark presumably with the sacred fire, an empty throne, and the king brandishing a bow, sitting on an elephant (badly stained), followed by other chiefs. Then a large palanquin on *hamsas* mounted on six wheels, pulled by men, is occupied by a prince between two ladies; finally, come princesses in palanquins surrounded by small people or children.

After the small door, a small panel shows a prince, or perhaps the king, imploring the favour of a god before going to war, lying prostrate before Shiva, close to an empty throne.

27. Small room. In a pond surrounded by steps, two boats can be seen sailing in waters full of fish, two of which have human heads. Two divers seem to be searching for a precious object, perhaps the shapeless block that can be seen above, carried shoulder-high on a sort of a throne. *Apsaras* and birds fly over this scene.

To the left, facing East, the relief illustrates a scene that was initially interpreted as an act of vandalism: some iconoclasts seem to be in the process of knocking over and breaking a statue of a woman, with a lot of ropes pulled by men and elephants.

Bosch (1933) proposed a better interpretation. Rather that trying to knock down and destroy something, the personages are busy ***freeing a woman from her prison in the mountain (228)***. Below her head they are digging open the rock with pickaxes, and the elephants pull it apart. Further down, they utilise the old technique of breaking rocks by fire and water (or vinegar). It seems that this scene relates the popular legend of a king or prince, who, when passing by a mountain, heard a female voice singing or moaning among the rocks. He asks his men to open the mountain and free the woman whom he eventually marries. From this action, spring water started to flow.

This would explain the relationship between this panel and the previous scene where people are diving in the water, which can be seen as the freed spring of fresh water becoming an object of veneration and of healing. One could also imagine that this somehow relates to the legend of the Leper King, illustrated in the nearby gallery, in which case the Shiva of the last panel

227 Sanctuary with three towers.

228 The legend of the freeing of a woman from her prison in the mountain.

229 The King fighting against a snake symbolic of a disease, possibly the leper.

230 *The legend of the Leper King. The king enthroned in his palace.*

of the low gallery would represent a simple healing *rishi*, in front of whom the king, whose life he had saved, would prostrate himself. But these are just working hypotheses.

28. Room between two towers. Here is a representation, on three registers, of the so-called *legend of the Leper King*, identified by Goloubew; it should be read from left to right. *A king is enthroned in his palace* (**230**), close to his spouse, surrounded by the court and dancing girls. He is then shown fighting an enormous *naga* (**229**), while below, the crowd comment on the event. The monster has vomited poison over him and therefore the king contracts leprosy. While himself remaining seated in his palace, he gives orders to his servants, who, descending a staircase, seem to hurry to the forest to consult the healing ascetics. Strange events take place in the forest: people are dying or fainting in the arms of others, or, too sick to walk themselves, are carried on people's shoulders, probably to see a saintly man, a *rishi*. Or are we dealing with the king's soldiers chasing away the people who are already there, in their haste to reach the saintly man and obtain the medicine for the king?

Next, women surrounding the sick king are examining his hands for the progression of the illness. Later still he can be seen lying down, with an ascetic standing at his side.

PREAH KHAN & TA PROHM

These two enormous temples were built between
the end of the 12th and the beginning of the
13th century by Jayavarman VII, who dedicated
Preah Khan to the his father and Ta Prohm to his
mother. Since both were of the Buddhist faith,
little of its iconography has escaped the
devastation of the Hinduist iconoclastic frenzy
which followed the death of the king. The Hindu
stories which had been simultaneously sculpted,
in accordance with Khmer syncretism, have not
been defaced.

Devoted to Hinduism, at Preah Khan, is the
Northern cloistered gallery, with reliefs narrating
the stories of Vishnu; particularly well executed is
the group of Krishna lifting Mount Govardhana,
and, in the Western gallery, reliefs depicting the
life of Vishnu and his *avatars*, as well as a
pediment with Vishnu sleeping on Ananta (*42*,
page 43). The pediments of the Western *gopura* of
the third enclosure have, on the East face, a scene
of people involved in a 'chess game on a boat'
(like at Angkor Wat and the Bayon), and on the
West face, an episode of the 'battle of Lanka'.

At Ta Prohm, even fewer narrative reliefs have
survived. Particularly noticeable is a pediment of
one tower from the Southwest quadrant court,
between the second and third enclosures, which
illustrates the **Great Departure** story of the
Buddha-to-be (*232*). While all the palace was
sleeping, four divinities supported the horse's
hoofs, to allow the prince to leave his father's
palace surreptitiously. **Stories from the Ramayana**
are also depicted (*231*). The exact episodes have
not yet been identified.

231 *A scene from the Ramanaya.*

232 *The Great Departure. Preah Khan. (Photo: M. Freeman)*

BANTEAY CHHMAR

This major temple is situated in the north-west corner of Cambodia, close to the Thai border. It is one of the most important monuments of Jayavarman VII, dedicated to his son Shridrakumara, and to four of his companions-in-arms who saved his life during a cruel battle. Built between the end of the 12th and the beginning of the 13th century, it is now in a very bad state of preservation, most of it being in ruins. The sculptural reliefs which survive are of high quality. Unfortunately, the site has not been accessible for several years, due to the political situation.

Only a few significant examples of reliefs are considered here, particularly the famous multi-armed Bodhisattvas. In fact, many images of *Avalokiteshvara* (*233*, *234*) decorate the walls of the Western gallery. They are shown with a single head but many arms. In the images with eight arms, a book, a rosary and a flask (*kundika*) are identifiable. They are flanked by worshippers, over whom celestial beings hover with lotuses and flower garlands.

There are also many reliefs of scenes from Hindu mythology and from the life of Jayavarman VII. One relief – quite deeply carved – depicts the story of *Brahma*, with his geese (*hamsas*), blessing an ascetic (*rishi*) who bows in front of him, while another plays the harp (*236*). Another panel tells the story of *Rahu*, the all-devouring mythical monster who had a predilection for eating the sun and the moon, thus causing eclipses; he is seen here fighting with a prince (*235*) and devouring an ox, a man and his cart (*237*).

233

234 *233 and 234: Avalokiteshvara. (Photos: M. Freeman)*

236 Harp players below worshippers of Brahma. (Photo: M. Freeman)

235 Rahu fighting with a prince. (Photo: M. Freeman)

237 Rahu devouring an ox, a man and his cart. (Photo: M. Freeman)

TERRACES OF THE ELEPHANTS & OF THE LEPER KING

These two buildings were constructed towards the end of the 12th century, during the reign of Jayavarman VII, on the eastern side of the Royal Palace, facing the so-called Royal square, from which the reliefs are clearly visible.

THE TERRACE OF THE ELEPHANTS

This wall, more then 300 m long, is carved in high relief with elephants in hunting scenes. Two elephants have seized a tiger, one holding its body and the other its thigh, while hunters hurl spears at a boar. A mahout drinks from his flask, oblivious of his master, touching his shoulder to remind him that he ought to leave some drink for the others. At the northern extremity of the terrace are located the most interesting reliefs depicting scenes of athletic games: horse riders fighting with spears, wrestlers, galloping chariots, gladiators; even **polo players** can be recognised (**100** and **101**, page 74). These could well be the entertainment that the king bestowed on his people in the square, a sort of forum, in front of the royal palace.

The interpretation of the reliefs at one extremity, modelled in a dynamic and powerful way, in higher relief, is problematic. There is a five-headed horse, shown frontally, surrounded by warriors with unusual hairstyles, and brandishing clubs. It is assumed that the scene takes place in a swamp, because the personages have their feet on lotus calyces. Small shaven-headed dwarves, looking frightened, cower between the legs of the horse; one of them holds a stick terminating in a cross. There is no definite reference for this story, although it has been suggested that the horse may represent Surya the sun, or the Bodhisattva Avalokiteshvara in the form of Balaha.

Behind the Terrace of the Elephants are the elegant **ponds of the Royal Palace**, with walls carved with friezes of decorative reliefs (**239**).

THE TERRACE OF THE LEPER KING

On top of this terrace, located immediately to the north of the Elephant Terrace, stood the statue of the so-called Leper king. However it represents neither a king nor a leper. Its mouth has fangs, and it therefore may represent a creature from hell.

Excavations have revealed that, behind the exterior wall, there is another, also entirely decorated (**238**). The reliefs, both of the exterior and interior walls, consist of superimposed registers. They illustrate rows of **various mythological beings** – *naga*, *Garuda*, Kumbhanda, etc., who inhabit Mount Meru, as well as a considerable number of demons, recognisable by their thick eyebrows and fangs, and perhaps representing personages from hell living below the sacred mountain.

238 *Mythological beings, including* naga, garuda *and Kumbhanda. Terrace of the Leper King. (Photo: M. Freeman)*

239 *Pool in the grounds of the Royal Palace decorated with reliefs of figures on the upper register and fish and water animals on the lower one. (Photo: M. Freeman)*

BANTEAY KDEI

This monument was built between the middle of the 12th and the early part of the 13th century, as a Mahayana Buddhist monastery, in the style of Bayon, with gates surmounted by *colossal faces* (*240*). As with all monuments of this type, the Buddhist iconography has been removed from the reliefs. Many of the lintels and pediments clearly show the contours of the image of Buddha which has carefully been effaced, in contrast to the surrounding worshippers and other decorative elements, which have remained untouched.

The monument is in a very precarious condition, but some pediments are intact. Noticeable are:

1. Gopura I West
Eastern face: pediment with the upper registers damaged, depicting people around a finely decorated building in which **Rama and Sita** stand

240 *The eastern entrance gopura with the face tower above.*

155

(*242*). It is surrounded by people in motion, possibly dancing, or rejoicing at the return of Rama to his palace of Ayodhya.

2. Gopura I North
Southern face: in the upper register Buddha in meditation; in the lower register a personage standing between two elephants.

3. Gopura II East
Pediment with four registers: at the top, a defaced image of the **Buddha in a decorated temple** (*241*); in the next, a figure, possibly the king, totally prostrate on the ground; at the base, two superimposed registers of worshippers.

Another pediment on three registers, depicts Buddha in meditation under the *bodhi* tree, between acolytes and *apsaras* in the upper register; below, are two rows of worshippers.

The northern tower, with Lokeshvara faces on the external enclosure, has interesting pediments, probably showing **Ramayana scenes** (*243*).

241 Pediment with the defaced image of the Buddha in a decorated temple, and a figure (the king?) prostrated on the ground. Gopura II E.

243 The northern tower of the external enclosure with Lokeshvara faces, has interesting pediments, probably taken from the Ramayana.

242 Pediment with Rama and Sita in their palace, after returning at Ayodhya. Gopura I W, E face.

TA NEI

This Buddhist temple was built towards the end of the 12th century by Jayavarman VII. The small *gopuras* of the exterior enclosure are probably slightly later. As with the other temples of Jayavarman VII, the reliefs narrating Buddhist stories have been defaced. However, several interesting pediments are still in place.

1. Gopura II East
Eastern face: *Lokeshvara* standing on a lotus between *apsaras* and flying personages; on the lower register some kneeling worshippers and devotees with large stomachs (*245*).

2. Gopura I South
Northern face, lower pediment with a large-scale kneeling *personage blessing two children* in a palace surrounded by *apsaras*; below, there is a row of worshippers (*246*).

3. Gopura I North
Southern face, a *horseman* brandishing a sword, above two registers of worshippers (*244*).

4. Central sanctuary
Northern face: a person standing in a junk makes a gesture of blessing, surrounded by flying figures with parasols. The pediment facing west represents, on two registers, the episode when the Buddha-to-be cuts off his hair, or is simply in a meditative state (defaced), while the lower register depicts his horse Balaha amongst worshippers.

Other pediments are much less well-preserved: some feature an erased image of the Buddha in meditation under the *bodhi* tree, amongst acolytes, or on a pedestal amongst worshippers.

245 Lokeshvara standing on a lotus in between apsaras *and flying personages; in the lower register some kneeling worshippers and preying persons with large stomachs. E gopura, E face.*

246 A large kneeling figure blessing two children in a palace amidst apsaras. *S gopura, N face, lower register.*

244 A horseman brandishing a sword, over two registers of worshippers. N gopura, S face.

NEAK PEAN

This temple (**248**), built by Jayavarman VII in the last quarter of the 12th century, was laden from the outset with intense symbolism. Its pool was intended to cleanse the sins of those who bathed therein, and the temple was to be like a boat crossing the ocean of the existence.

It is finely decorated, and its narrative reliefs are focused on the **Bodhisattva Lokeshvara** who figures in the large images sculpted on the four doors of the shrine of this circular island (**247**). Above each image there is a pediment (much dilapidated) narrating an episode in the life of Buddha: to the East, the Cutting of the hair; to the North, the Great departure; to the West, Buddha in meditation under the *bodhi* tree; the Southern pediment is completely eroded. The four small chapels surrounding the square pool have multiple pediments also depicting Buddhist motifs (**249** and **250**).

In the pool surrounding the shrine, may be seen the statue representing the legend of the Balaha horse (**88**, page 65).

247 False door of the central sanctuary. West face.

248 View of the main shrine at the centre of the pool. (Photo: M. Freeman)

249 *Pediment of southern chapel.*

250 *Pediment of northern chapel.*

PREAH PALILAY

This temple, located in the northwest quadrant of Angkor Thom, is of the Theravada Buddhist faith. It was probably built during the reign of Dharanindravarman II (1150-1160), who promoted Buddhism. Although his efforts were ephemeral, some 30 years later, his son Jayavarman VII was to institute Buddhism as the state religion.

The temple is preceded by a *naga* bridge, leading to a Buddha statue of colossal size erected much later. The temple which is of cruciform plan, is surrounded by one enclosure wall with a single *gopura*, on the east (**251**). The latter has a cruciform plan elongated along the north-south axis. The Eastern and Western sides have principal and secondary entrances with pediments, while the North and South faces have none, and are merely walls with gables adorned with pediments.

From a study of the architectural and iconographic elements, it seems that although the main sanctuary was built in the second half of the 12th century, the *gopura* may have been added later, during the 13th century. These two distinct phases (Glaize, 1940) are evident from the walls ending abruptly against the gables of the *gopura*, which seems to have been built astride the earlier laterite enclosure wall, visible deeply set inside the walls of the building. The iconography of the reliefs shows some unusual elements, while the execution shows variable standards.

The Buddhist images of this temple survived the destruction which occurred after the death of Jayavarman VII, and the following thesis has been proposed to explain this phenomenon. Despite the dominance of Hinduism during most of the Angkorean period, Theravada Buddhism was tolerated from the end of the 9th century, when Yashovarman permitted the building of Tep Pranam, in the shadow of the Royal palace. The iconoclastic fever of Jayavarman VIII was directed against the Mahayanist temples, but spared the Theravada icons. This tolerance was also extended to the temples known as N.486 and temple X of Preah Pithu, both within the walls of

251 *The single gopura of Preah Palilay is on the East side.*

Angkor Thom, although, of course, they may have been built or modified in the late 13th century or even later. The main shrine of Preah Palilay was studied by Marchal in 1922, and the *gopura* by Glaize in 1940.

The reliefs of Preah Palilay are amongst the few surviving Buddhist images. The most significant reliefs are those in the cruciform *gopura* described in detail below, although others, now lying on the ground seem to originate from the sanctuary.

1. Sanctuary

Marchal (1922) described and photographed a pediment representing Buddha receiving the king of the *Nagas*, recognisable by a crown in the shape of a *naga* head, and another figure with a three-pointed crown. The Buddha is seated in the earth-touching position (*bhumisparsa mudra*), surrounded by *devaputtas*, under the *bodhi* tree;

in the register below, two rows of three worshippers are separated by an indistinct central figure; in the lower register there is the usual row of worshippers. Only a few of the sanctuary lintels have survived, the one with Indra on his three-headed elephant being the best-preserved.

2. Gopura Eastern face

Over the main entrance door. The pediment shows a large **standing Buddha** (**252**), in a sinuous pose on a pedestal, surrounded by acolytes and flying beings; two rows of **worshippers** fill the lower register. On the lintel below, is a representation of the **dying Buddha** (**84**, see page 65), lying on his left side, with disciples at his side.

Over the secondary entrance to the North, a pediment relates the **miracle of the Parilyyaka** forest, where Buddha receives the offerings of the animals in the forest (elephants, monkeys, peacock), and a bowl from a standing figure (**83**, page 65). It was this episode of his life which gave the name to the temple, Palilay deriving from Parilyyaka, the forest to where the Buddha retreated, after leaving Kosambi, and where an elephant ministered to him.

252 *Standing Buddha. Eastern face of the gopura.*

3. Gopura Northern face

On the plain wall, are two overlapping pediments. In the upper register of the lower one, the seated Buddha subdues with his right hand the **mad elephant Nalagiri** (**87**, page 65).

On the upper pediment, the figure of Buddha seated in the *dhyana mudra* is being shaped in stone by the chisels of two sculptors; a row of worshippers complete the lower register.

4. Gopura Western face

Over the main door there is a pediment with a **family scene**, sculpted in three registers (**253**). In the lowest, there are three elephants passing through the forest from right to left, followed by people on foot. The second animal is guided by his mahout, while the third carries a royal personage on his chair. In the middle register are two crowned ladies holding their children, and on the upper register is Buddha, standing between

two fans, with both arms lowered, apparently to touch the heads of the children.

Over the northern door, the top register of the pediment shows **Buddha**, with a broad smiling face, seated under a tree in the *rajalalitasana* position with one knee and his right arm raised (**79**, page 63). He is flanked by two kneeling personages. In the middle register, are four figures seated amongst trees, some carrying a pole at the ends of which bundles are hanging; at the centre are conical items, presumably gifts. The lower register shows the usual worshippers alternating with trees. This may represent Buddha accepting the offerings of Sujata.

5. Gopura Southern face

On the plain wall, there are two overlapping pediments illustrating **Buddha in meditation**: in the upper pediment he is represented in the *dhyana mudra*, while in the lower he is in the

253 *Top: Elephants in the forest occupy the lower register of the pediment from the Western face of the gopura, Preah Palilay.*

254 *Above: Buddha in meditation. Upper pediment, Southern face of the gopura, Preah Palilay.*

255 *Lintel from temple 't' showing the Churning of the Ocean of Milk.*

256 *A lintel from temple 'u' also illustrates the same story as above.*

bhumisparsa mudra; in both instances, rows of worshippers appear in the lower registers (**81** and **82**, page 63).

Not far from Preah Palilay, Marchal (1918), described another interesting pediment from a Buddhist location in the northern direction towards Tep Pranam, that he defined as 'Terrace D'. The relief shows, within a trilobate *naga* frame, a Buddhist story in three registers: the top depicts Buddha seated in meditation on a pedestal, with a stylised *bodhi* tree and an attendant on either side. In the middle register is a row of worshippers, and in the lower, Mara's army on elephants assaulting the Buddha.

PREAH PITHU

This name refers to a complex of temples and terraces located in the north-eastern corner of the Royal Square of Angkor Thom, most of them in ruins. The etymology of the name seems to derive from the Khmer pronunciation of Vidhura, one of the many Bodhisattvas preceding the historical Buddha. His adventures are told in the *Vidhurapandita Jataka*, the penultimate of the last ten *jatakas*, preceding the *Vessantara Jataka*.

Glaize described them in detail in his 1944 guide (new edition, 1993) classifying them by number, instead of the customary letters. They can be equated as follows: 1st = t, 2nd = u, 3rd = x, 4th = v, 5th = y. All seem to have been built and richly decorated in the Angkor Wat style, although temple 't' is probably of the Bayon period. Their dates range from the 12th to the 13th century. With the exception of temple 'x', they all are Hinduist.

1. Temple 't' (first temple of Glaize)
There are no *in situ* reliefs, but on the ground, a fragment of a lintel with a poorly-executed ***Churning of the Ocean of Milk*** (***255***).

2. Temple 'u' (second temple of Glaize)
The lintel of the shrine facing north carries a finely carved representation of the ***Churning of the Ocean of Milk*** (***256***). There is no pivoting pole, and Vishnu sits astride the *naga* Vasuki; below is the turtle surmounted by Indra's animals, born from the churning: the horse Uccaihshravas and the elephant Airavata, and two figures in human shape, probably *apsaras*.

The Western lintel depicts a *Trimurti*; the Southern lintel, Shiva as an ascetic with his left arm raised; and the Eastern, Brahma on a *kala*. The lintels of the Western *gopura* are carved with a dancing Shiva, and Vishnu on Garuda.

3. Temple 'x' (third temple of Glaize), also called Ta Tuot (Marchal 1918). (***257***).
Built before the 'abandonement' of Angkor, this temple is characteristic of the Theravada monasteries of the Angkor area (Giteau, 1975). The sculptural decoration was probably added later, introducing post-Angkorean iconographic elements. The reliefs are either *in situ* in the central sanctuary, or in fragments at the base of the high terrace.

The central shrine and the preceding small antechambers are decorated with ***several Buddha figures***, all in the *bhumisparsa (Maravijaya) mudra* (***258***), sometimes accompanied by worshippers. On the lintel of the second door facing East, Buddha is surrounded by worshippers who have a sort of a halo around their heads. His *ushnisa* terminates in a pointed flame, in typical Thai fashion (***259***). The upper part of the shrine walls are carved with a frieze on two registers with many seated Buddhas dressed in Angkorean style.

257 Monument 'x', third temple of Glaize, view of the temple.

258 Monument 'x' Buddha figures, all in the bhumisparsa (Maravijaya) mudra.

However, the heads, with very arched eyebrows and very circular smiling lips, are of the post-Bayon or later type.

The sculptural fragments on the ground are varied in iconography, but are too fragmentary for precise classification. Worth noticing is the reconstructed pediment, brought to the Conservatory of Siem Reap (**78**, page 61), illustrating the 'Cutting of the hair' (Giteau, 1975). In it, the figures around the Buddha have hair styles and crowns strongly influenced by the Thai style of Ayutthaya. Above the Buddha, a *devata* approaches the scene descending vertically, in the Chinese fashion. In fact, according to Giteau (ibid), in classical Khmer art, such flying *devatas* come down from the sky horizontally, while in the Bayon period, they do so diagonally, according to a Chinese tradition already introduced in the reliefs of the northeast quadrant of Angkor Wat. The Buddha's equerry, Chandaka, is portrayed movingly, leaning his head on the horse Kanthaka whom he knows will die of sorrow upon losing his master.

By comparing these iconographic elements with those from Wat Nokor, it is reasonable to suppose that these Buddhist reliefs may have been carved in the 16th century.

4. Temple 'v' (fourth temple of Glaize)
This strongly-built small temple is noticeable for a large *linga*, still in place in the northern antechamber of the cella, where it was probably originally located (**260**).There are a number of sculptural fragments on the ground, mainly *nagas*.

5. Temple 'y' (fifth temple of Glaize)
This small temple on a low hill presents some interesting reliefs. The Northern half-pediment facing West shows the ***victory of Krishna over the asura Bana*** (**261**). The Southern half-pediment facing West shows **the Three Steps of Vishnu** (**44**, page 43). The Southern pediment illustrates the fight of Sugriva and Valin.

259 Buddha surrounded by worshippers who have a sort of a halo around the heads, while his ushnisa *terminates in a pointed flame. Monument 'x'.*

260 Monument 'v', showing the linga *still in place.*

261 The victory of Krishna over the asura Bana. Monument 'y', *northern half-pediment facing West.*

WAT NOKOR

This temple, formerly called Vat Nagar, is located near Kompong Cham, in eastern central Cambodia. It was built by provincial artists in the style classified as late Bayon, at the beginning of the 13th century. Initially a Mahayana Buddhist temple, it was not abandoned at the end of the Angkorean period, but became a Theravada sanctuary. It was restored several times, both in its foundations and its reliefs, mostly during the 16th century, when the superstructure of the main tower was rebuilt in the shape of a *stupa*.

It was studied by Parmentier in 1916, and later by Giteau who analysed the narrative reliefs in 1967. Today, part of it has been included in a Buddhist temple. The Western entrance is flanked by a picturesque row of sugar palm trees (*262*).

As discussed previously, Buddhist iconography is rare in the 13th century, following a systematic campaign of destruction. It seems plausible that the fervour of King Ang Chang in the 16th century, not only led to the completion of the reliefs of the north-east quadrant of Angkor Wat, but had an influence on the pediments of this temple and introduced a new imagery.

Western pediment

The pediment representing the ***Sleep of Women*** (*76*, page 61) is in two registers. At the top are three figures in a pavilion, the head of the central one surmounted by a thin flame or point. They

262 Western entrance to the temple, showing the pagoda like superstructure.

are seated in the *rajalalitasana* position, and looking sleepy. At either side of the building are two kneeling women with their hands on their faces, also looking as though they are asleep. In the lower register there is a row of 13 women, seated half-kneeling, in disarray, holding their head in one arm, with closed eyes – perhaps they are sleeping dancing girls.

This pediment seems to show the last night of the Buddha-to-be in his royal household, amidst the court ladies and dancers. After giving them and his wife and son a last glance, the Future Buddha secretly left the palace for good.

Northern pediment

Undoubtedly this story takes place after the above, since it represents the ***Great Departure*** (*77*, page 61). The composition is also in two registers. The upper one contains the principal scene: the Future Buddha is riding his horse Kanthaka, going from right to left, surrounded by four insignia and umbrella carriers, three of whom seem to be under his horse and one behind it. Note that none of them is supporting the horse's hoofs, as in the original story and in later Cambodian tradition. The lower register illustrates only a row of worshippers.

Southern pediment

This follows the previous story, and shows the *Future Buddha freeing his horse and squire*. (*75*, page 61). The composition is in three registers. The Future Buddha, having dismounted from his loyal horse, is sitting in the *virasana* position and, with his left hand, cuts the horse's bridles with his sword, setting him free (but he will die of sorrow). Due to the erosion of the rock, the Buddha might also be cutting his own hair. Two tiered parasols frame this scene, and two worshippers kneel at either side. The middle register shows the horse still saddled and his squire holding the bridles. The lower register presents seven worshippers, with crown and chignon-cover, alternating with large lotus buds hanging from the roof.

The way the horse is sculpted differs from that of the Northern pediment and from Preah Pithu, monument 'x', where the animal is lying down and attended to by his squire; both these examples are strongly influenced by Thai art.

Eastern pediment

It is difficult to read this pediment of the *Buddha's enlightenment* (*80*, page 63) because it is now inside the later *vihara*. Moreover, it has been plastered, painted and covered with gold leaf. It does not have registers and the triangular lobate space is occupied, at the centre, by a pavilion on a very tall base. This offers shelter to the Buddha seated in the *bhumisparsa mudra*. His head has the *ushnisa* surmounted by a straight flame. At the base kneels Brah Dharani, the Goddess of the Earth, in response to the Buddha's call, witnessing his enlightenment. She twists her hair to produce the flood that will drown the army of demons that the evil *Mara* has sent to destroy the Buddha. To both sides of the tall pavilion's base, are multitudes of monsters and soldiers menacing

the Buddha, some shooting arrows which are transformed into inoffensive birds.

Giteau (ibid) has noticed discrepancies in the style and techniques of the reliefs. The composition is sometimes lifeless and the costumes differ, suggesting that they were sculpted at different times. She believes that the pediment illustrating *The sleep of women* may be the oldest and contemporary with the original building (early 13th century) while the other three may have been made to replace pediments defaced during the 13th century.

There are also stylistic analogies with the reliefs from the north-east quadrant of Angkor Wat dated by Cœdès to between1546 to 1564. This dating is further reinforced by the inscription commemorating the digging, at Wat Nokor, of new foundations in 1566. These three pediments must have been sculpted between the middle and the end of the 16th century, during the reoccupation of Angkor by King Ang Cham.

In the Western *gopura*, there are two well-executed pediments with large images of *Avalokiteshvara* (*263*) framed by the lobate mould of the *naga* terminating, at both ends, with exceptionally large heads. Stylistically they are very similar to the reliefs of Neak Pean.

TA PROHM OF BATI

The foundations of this temple, located some 20 km south of Phnom Penh, close to Tonlé Bati, probably date to the 12-13th centuries. It is a monument of modest size, mostly in laterite and in a poor state of preservation (*264*). However, it is remarkable for the presence of a relief narrating the death of the Buddha, the *Mahaparinirvana*. The Buddha reclines on his right side, with his head raised on pillows, with two acolytes manifesting their sorrow. Also a Buddha in meditation under a three-stepped parasol is represented here. According to their stylistic characteristics, in the opinion of Giteau (1975), these sculptural reliefs seem to have been executed in the 16th century. These exists beside a possibly earlier Vishnuite relief.

In the garden now surrounding the temple, are a lintel with the **Churning of the Ocean of Milk**, of questionable date (*265*), and a lintel with a family on a typical Khmer cart pushed by a horse, surrounded by people carrying parasols, perhaps refering to **some episode of the Ramayana (266)**.

Detached from the main temple is a shrine, later absorbed into the Buddhist monastery whose a pediment depicts **Vishnu over a treble lintel** of worshippers (*267*).

264 *The laterite temple of Ta Prohm of Bati.*

265 *Churning of the Ocean of Milk.*

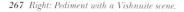

266 *Lintel showing an unidentified* Ramayana *scene.*

267 *Right: Pediment with a Vishnuite scene.*

263 *Opposite: The Avalokiteshvara of Wat Nokor is similar in style to that of Neak Pean.*

Bibliography

Unless otherwise stated, the publications listed here are available or can be obtained from specialised book shops at the time of going to press. Many are in French. The publications listed under 'Further reading' can be found mainly in institutional libraries.

GENERAL ON KHMER ART

The two books in French by Madelaine Giteau, for long Curator of the National Museum of Phnom Penh, *Les Khmers*, *Bibliothèque des Arts, Paris, 1965*, and *Angkor*, *Bibliothèque des Arts, Paris, 1976*, are pleasant to read and a very good introduction to the art and life of the Khmers, presented in a romantic way. Regrettably, they are out of print. The same applies to one of the more comprehensive books (in French), by J. Boisselier in the series on Southeast Asia: *Le Cambodge*, *Picard, Paris, 1966*.

Angkor by A. Le Bonheur (in French), *1989*, presents a complete and systematic development of Khmer history and art, but is unfortunately also out of print. The accurate survey *Angkor* by Claude Jacques (in French), *Bordas, 1993*, reflects the most modern views, sustained by the author's extensive knowledge of epigraphy. The revised English edition *Angkor: Cities and Temples* has recently been published by Thames and Hudson. The graphic explanation of the growth and expansion of the cities under Kings Yashovarman I, Rajendravarman, and Suryavarman I, is particularly well rendered.

Three small publications are essential. The first is the English translation of *The Customs of Cambodia* from the notes written in late 13th century by Chou Ta Kuan, re-edited by the *Siam Society* of Bangkok, in *1992*. The second is the classic, excellent paperback *Angkor, An Introduction* by G. Cœdès, reprinted several times by *Oxford University Press*. The third, dealing mainly with the fascinating story of the exploration and discovery of Angkor, is the small paperback *Angkor* by Bruno Dagens, *Thames and Hudson, 1989*.

The very successful book by P. Rawson *The Art of Southeast Asia*, *Thames and Hudson, 1967*, despite being a rather unstructured overview, is well illustrated, and presents Khmer art within a regional context. A more coherent text is the one, in French, by L. Frederic printed in 1994. There are various photographic essays such as *Angkor, The Hidden Glories* by M. Freeman and R.Warner, *Houghton Mifflin, London 1990* and Mark Standen *A Passage through Angkor*, *Asia Books, 1992*.

HISTORY AND CULTURE

For a comprehensive picture of Khmer people and their culture one must refer to *A History of Cambodia* by David Chandler, *Westview Press, 1992*, and the readable survey *The Khmers*, by Ian Mabbet and David Chandler, *Blackwell, 1995*. To cover the pre-history and early history of the wider area is Charles Higham's *The Archaeology of Mainland Southeast Asia*, *Cambridge University Press, 1989*.

Three substantial books dealing with the history of the area are George Cœdès *The Indianised states of Southeast Asia*, *East-West Center Book, University Press of Hawaii, 1968*, the work by D.G.E. Hall *History of South-East Asia*, *MacMillan,1981*, and the *Cambridge History of Southeast Asia*, edited by N. Tarling for *Cambridge University Press,1992*.

NARRATIVE RELIEFS

Only one book, by A. Le Bonheur is available exclusively on the topic of Khmer reliefs – *Of Gods, Kings and Men*, *Serindia Publications, London 1995*. Unfortunately, the illustrations do not do full justice to the original photographs by Jaroslav Poncar. Recently, the second volume (only) of the colossal work by Finot, Cœdès and Goloubev, *Le Temple d'Angkor*, has been reprinted by *S.D.I. Publications, Bangkok,1995;* regrettably, its cost makes it inaccessible to most pockets.

MYTHS AND LEGENDS

The books suggested for this subject are limited to popular editions currently available. In the 'Penguin classics' series are: *Hindu Myths*, by W. Doniger O'Flaherty (1975)*; The Bhagavad Gita*, edited by J. Mascaro (1962)*;* and *Buddhist Scriptures* edited by E. Conze (1959). Extremely informative is *The Ramayana of Valmiki*, brilliantly edited by R.P. Golmnad, *Princeton Library of Asian Translations, 1984-90.* An elucidating survey is *Many Ramayanas*, edited by P. Richman, *University of California Press, 1991.*

GUIDES

Some excellent guides are available. The most comprehensive and detailed is the one (in French) by M. Glaize, *Les Monuments du Groupe d'Angkor*, originally written in 1944, updated and reprinted in *1993* by *Maisonneuve*. The compact guide by D. Rooney, *Angkor, An Introduction to the Temples*, *Odessey, 1994,* is also quite useful.

CD-ROMS

To date three CD-ROMs are on the market, two in French and one in English.
•	*Angkor, Cité Royale*, by J. Friedman, Editions *Infogrames Multimedia, Villeurbane-cedex, France.*
•	*Angkor*, 10 Siècles de Fascination by F. Cerezales. *Comme un voyage, Paris, 1997.*
•	*Khmer Mythology*, by V. Roveda, *21st Century Media Ltd, Hove, 1997.*

FURTHER READING

Alvares S.H., *'L'iconographie du temple de Bakong de sa fondation au XIII siècle'*. *Histoire de l'Art, No.20, 1992.*

A.P.S.A.R.A., *Angkor, Past, Present and Future*, *Unesco, 1996.*

Bath A. and Bergaigne A., *Inscriptions Sanskrite du Champa et du Cambodge*, *Paris, 1885-93.*

Benisti M., *'Rapports entre le premier art khmer et l'art indien'*. EFEO, *Mémoires archéologiques V, 1970.*

Beylie de, General, *Photographie des reliefs de Banteay Chhmar*, *Musée Guimet* 1913.

Bhandari C.M., *Saving Angkor*, *White Orchid Books, Bangkok, 1995.*

Bhattacharya K., *'Les Religions brahmaniques dans l'ancien Cambodge d'après l'épigraphie et l'iconographie'*. *BEFEO XLIX, 1961.*

Boisselier J., *Asie du Sud-Est, Tome I, Le Cambodge*, *Picard, Paris, 1966.*

Boisselier J., *'Pouvoir royal et symbolisme architectural: Neak Pean et son importance pour la royauté angkorienne'*, *Arts Asiatiques XXXI, 1970.*

Boisselier J., *Le Cambodge*, *Paris, Picard, 1966.*

Bonn G., *Angkor, Toleranz in Stein*, *Dumont, 1996 (in German).*

Bosch, F.D.K., *'Un Bas-Relief du Bayon'*, *BEFEO, XXXI, 1931-32.*

Bosch, F.D.K., *'Le Temple d'Angkor Vat'*, *BEFEO, XXXII, 1933.*

Chou Ta-kuan (Zhou Daguan), *The Customs of Cambodia*, *The Siam Society, Bangkok, 1992.*

Cœdès G., *Le Temple d'Angkor Vat*, *Paris 1932 (in folio).*

Cœdès G., *'La date d'execution des deux bas-reliefs tardifs d' Angkor Vat'*, *Journal Asiatique, 1962.*

Cœdès G., 1989/92, *'Articles sur le pays khmer*, reprint of 63 papers from *EFEO.*

Cœdès G. *Angkor*, *Oxford University Press, re-issue 1990.*

Comaille J., et Cœdès G. *Le Bayon d'Angkor Thom. Bas-reliefs publiés par le soin de la Commission archéologigue de l'Indochine,* Paris, Leroux, 1910 and 1914.

Coral-Rémusat, G. de, *L'Art Khmer, les grandes étapes de son évolution* in *Etudes d'art et d'ethnologie Asiatiques, Vanoest, Paris, 1951.*

Dagens B., '*Etude sur l'iconographie du Bayon (frontons et linteaux)' Arts Asiatiques XIX, 1969.*

Dagens B., *Angkor, la forêt de pierre. Gallimard 'Decouvertes' No.64, 1989.*

Dagens B., *Angkor, Heart of an Asian Empire, Thames and Hudson, London 1955.*

Dagens B., '*Etude iconographique de quelques fondations de l'époque de Suryavarman I', Arts Asiatiques, 17, 1968.*

Delvert J., *Le Cambodge, PUF 'Que sais-je? No.2080, 1983.*

Deydier H., '*Etude d'iconographie buddhique et brahmique', BEFEO, XLVI, 1952-54.*

Dufour H., *Le Bayon d'Angkor Thom, Ministère de l'Instruction publique et des Beaux Arts, Paris, Leroux 1913. (Folio).*

Dumarcay J. and Smithies M., *Cultural sites of Burma, Thailand and Cambodia, Oxford University Press, Kuala Lumpur, 1995.*

Dumont R., '*Trois examples d'architecture khmère', Dossier d'Histoire et archeologie, No.125, 1988.*

Filliozat J., '*Le symbolisme du monument du Phnom Bakheng', BEFEO XLIV, 1954.*

Filliozat J., *Le temple de Hari dans le Harivarsa, Arts Asiatiques, Paris 1961, VIII, fasc.3, p.196.*

Filliozat J., '*Sur le civaisme et le bouddhisme du Cambodge', BEFEO, 1981.*

Finot L., Goloubew V., et Cœdès G., *Le temple d'Angkor Vat, EFEO, Mem. Archeol. II, 1927-32.*

Finot L., Parmentier H. et Goloubew V., '*Le temple d'Ishvarapura (Banteay Srei)', Publ. de l'EFEO, Mémoires archaélogiques, I, Paris, 1926.*

Fontein J., *The sculpture of Indonesia, Nat. Gall. of Art, Washington, H.N. Abrams Inc., NY, 1990.*

Frederic L., *L'art de l'Inde et de l'Asie du Sud-Est,* Flammarion, 1994.

Geoffroy-Shneider B., Jaques C., and Zewphir T., *L'ABCdaire d'Angkor et l'art Khmer, Flammarion, Paris, 1997.*

Giteau M., '*Iconographie du Cambodge postangkorien,' EFEO, Vol. C, Paris 1975.*

Giteau M., *Une representation de la Bhiksatanamurti de Shiva à Angkor Vat', Arts Asiatiques, XI/1, 1965.*

Giteau M., *Note sur les frontons du sanctuaire central de Vat Nagar, Arts Asiatiques, XVI, 1967.*

Giteau M., *Histoire d'Angkor, Kailash, Paris, 1996.*

Glaize M., '*La gopura de Prah Palilai', BEFEO, XL, 1940.*

Glaize M., *Le Guide d'Angkor: les monuments du groupe d'Angkor, Paris Maisonneuve, 1963.*

Goloubew V., '*Le cheval Balaha', BEFEO, XXVII, 1927.*

Grison P., *Angkor au centre du monde, Dervy-Livres, Paris, 1980.*

Groslier G., '*Le temple de Phnom Cisor', Arts et archéologie khmers, Vol.1, 1921-22.*

Groslier B.P., *Le temple de Prah Vihear, Arts et archéologie khmers, Vol.1, 1921-22.*

Groslier B.P., *Indochine, carrefour des arts, Paris, Michel 1960.*

Groslier B.Ph., *L'Indochine, in L'Art dans le Monde, Edit. A.Michel, Paris, 1961.*

Groslier B.Ph., '*La cité hydraulique angkorienne', BEFEO, LXVI, 1979.*

Higham C., *The Archaeology of Mainland Southeast Asia, Cambridge University Press, 1989.*

Jacq-Hergoulc'h M., *L'armement et l'organisation de l'armée khmère, Paris PUF, Publ. du Musée Guimet, Recherches et documents d'art et d'archéologie XII, 1970.*

Jacques C. & Dumont R., *Angkor, Paris, Bordas 1990.*

Jacques C., *Angkor: Cities and Temples*, London, Thames and Hudson, 1997.

Jessup H.I. and Zephir T., *Angkor et dix siecles d'art khmer*, Réunion des Musées Nationaux, 1997.

Klokke M.J., *Tantri reliefs on Javanse candi*, KITLV Press, Leiden, 1993.

Lan Sunnary, *Etude iconographique du temple khmer de Thommanon (Dhammananda)*, Arts Asiatiques, 25, 1972, p.177.

Le Bonheur A., *Cambodge. Angkor. Temples en peril*, Paris, Hershcer, 1989.

Le Bonheur A., *Of Gods, Kings, and Men*, Serindia, London, 1995.

Mannikka E., *Angkor Wat: Meaning through measurement*, University of Michigan dissertation, 1985.

Mannikka E., *Angkor Wat, Time, Space, and Kingship*, University of Hawaii Press, 1996.

Marchal H., *'Monuments secondaires et terrasses buddhiques d'Angkor Thom'*, BEFEO, XVIII, 1918.

Marchal H., *'Le temple de Preah Palilai'*, BEFEO, XXII, 1922.

Marchal H., *Sur le monument 486 d'Angkor Thom*, BEFEO, XXV, 1925.

Marchal H., *The temples d'Angkor*, 5th edit., A. Guillot, Paris 1955.

Martini F., *'En marge du Ramayana cambodgien'*, BEFEO, XXXVIII, 1938.

Martini F., *La gloire de Rama, Ramakerti*, Collection Le Monde Indien, Paris, 1978.

Mazzeo D. and Silvi Antonini C., *Civilta Khmer*, Mondadori, Milano/Tokyo, 1972. (in Italian).

Mazzeo D. and Silvi Antonini C., *Ancient Cambodia*, Grosset & Dunlap, New York, 1978.

Mus P., *'Le sourir d'Angkor'*, Artibus Asiae XXIV, 1961.

Nafilyan G., *'Angkor Vat. Description graphique du temple'*, EFEO, Mem. Archeol. IV, 1969.

Paris P., *'L'importance rituelle du Nord-Est et ses applications en Indochine'*, BEFEO, XLII, 1941.

Parmentier H., *L'art khmer classique, Monuments du quadrant nord-east*, Publication de l'Ecole Française d'Extrême Orient, Paris, 1939.

Parmentier H., *Wat Nokor*, BEFEO, XVI, 1916-17.

Parmentier H., *'Les bas-reliefs de Banteai Chhmar'*, BEFEO, X, No.1, 1910.

Przyluski J., *'La legende de Rama dans les bas reliefs d'Angkor-Vat'*, Art et Archeologie Khmere, Vol.1, 1921-22.

Przyluski J., *'The legend of Krishna at Bayon'*, The Yearbook of Oriental Art and Culture, 1927.

Przyluski J., *'La légende de Krishna dans les bas-reliefs d'Angkor Vat'*, Revue des Arts Asiatiques, V/II, 1928.

Pym C., *The ancient civilization of Angkor*, Mentor Book, 1968.

Ramayana of Valmiki, translated by Hari P. Sastri, Shanti Sadan, London, 1992.

Rawson P., *The art of Southeast Asia*, Thames and Hudson, 1967.

Ribeau M., *Angkor, the serenity of Buddhism*, Thames and Hudson, 1993.

Rodriguez N., *'Variation autour d'un thème iconographique: Arjuna et le Kirata'*. EASAA, 6th Internat. Conf, Leiden, 1996.

Stencel R. & Moron E., *'Astronomy and Cosmology at Angkor Wat*, Science, No.193, 1978.

Sterlin H., *Angkor, Architecture universelle*, Office du Livre, Fribourg, 1970.

Stern Ph., *Les Monuments khmers du style du Bayon*, Publ. Musée Guimet, IX, 1965.

Thierry S., *Les Khmers, Le Seuil*, Paris, 1974.

Zephir T., *L'art khmer*, in *L'art de l'Asie du Sud-East*, Citadelles & Mazenod, Paris 1994.

Zephir T., *L'empire des rois khmers*, Gallimard, Paris, 1997.

Glossary of Khmer Terms and Principal Mythological Characters

Agni   The god of fire. Guardian of the Southeast.

Airavata   Sacred elephant and vehicle of the god Indra. Also one of the elephants that supports the four quarters of the world.

Amrita   The nectar of immortality.

Ananta   The multi-headed serpent on which Vishnu rests during his withdrawal from the world.

Anantasayin   Epithet of Vishnu when resting on Ananta.

Angada   The monkey warrior son of Valin.

Angkor   The capital (from *nagara*).

Apsaras   Celestial water nymphs, wives of the *Gandharvas* (celestial musicians).

Arjuna   The king of the Haihayas, of the Pandava tribe. Pandu, his real father, chose Indra as his 'godly' father.

Ascetics   Sages who practised austerities.

Ashram   A retreat, a hermitage.

Asuras   Devilish monster. Involved in fights with the *devas*.

Avalokiteshvara   'Lord of compassion', the most venerated *Bodhisattva*.

Ayodhaya   The capital of Koshala which was ruled by Dasharahta, Rama's father.

Balaha   Horse who saved the merchant Simhala and embodied one of the previous incarnations of the Buddha.

Balarama   Brother of Vishnu.

Bali   A king of the demons.

Bana   *Asura* who fought Krishna. Son of Bali.

Banteay   Citadel, temple with enclosure walls.

baray   Pond or reservoir.

Beng   Pond.

Bhima   One of the Pandava protagonists from the Battle of Kurukshetra.

bhumisparsa mudra   Gesture of the Buddha in which his left hand is in his lap and his right hand touches the ground.

Bishma   Son of Santanu and 'grandfather' of the Kauravas.

Bodhisattva   Being called to obtain Enlightenment, but who delays it through compassion for suffering beings.

Brah Dharani   Goddess of the Earth, who witnessed the Buddha's enlightenment.

Brahma   Member of the Hindu trinity with Shiva and Vishnu. Known as the Creator of the Universe.

Chakravartin   Indian royal title meaning 'universal sovereign'.

Chandaka   The Buddha's squire who accompanied him initially when he left the palace to seek enlightenment.

Chandrahasa   The glittering scimitar, Ravana's sword, which he received from Shiva as a boon.

Chitralekha   Usha's friend.

Citragupta   The record keeper of human deeds and misdeeds.

Dasharatha   King of Kosala and father of Rama.

Davantaka   A *rakasha* warrior.

Devadatta   Envious cousin of the Buddha.

Devaputtas   Flying male celestial beings.

Devaraja   'God who is king', the divinity who rules the country.

Deva   A god.

Devata   Female divinity.

Devi   Title given to Parvati, wife of Shiva.

Dhritarashtra   The blind king of the Kauravas.
Draupadi   Wife of the Arjuna from the *Mahabharata*.
Duryodhana   The wicked eldest son of King Dhritarashtra who precipitated the Battle of Kurukshetra and fought with Bhima.
Dvarapala   Guardian divinities of doors and gateways.

Ganesha   The elephant god and son of Shiva. Also known as Ganapati.
Garbhaghra   Inner chamber of the shrine.
Garuda   King of the birds, vehicle of Vishnu.
Gopura   Large doorway to the temple, often enlarged into a small building.

Hamsa   Sacred goose (or swan), vehicle of Brahma.
Hanuman   White monkey general with magical powers.
Harihara   A combination of Shiva (on the right) and Vishnu (on the left).
Hevajra   Tantric divinity.
Hiranyakasipu   Demon who was slain by Vishnu.

Indra   The king of the Gods and guardian of the East.
Indrajit   Son of Ravana.
Janaka   King of Mithila, father of Sita.
Jatayus   The king of vultures.

Kabandha   *Asura* or demon slain by Rama.
Kailasa   Sacred mountain abode of Shiva.
kala   Face commonly appearing over doorways, perhaps representing Rahu.
Kalanemi   An *asura* enemy of the gods.
Kaliya   *Naga* wounded by Krishna.
kalpa   A cycle of time.
Kama   God of love.
Kamsa   Uncle of Krishna who attempted to kill him when he was young.
Kanthaka   The Buddha's horse.
Karma   Actions or deeds which determine a being's subsequent existences.
Kaundinya   The first Indian prince.
Kauravas   The tribe who fought the Pandavas in the Battle of Kurukshetra.

Ketu   Monster who creates comets and meteors, born from the tail of Rahu.
Kinnari   Bird maidens.
Kiratas   A race of hunters.
Kompong   Rural village.
Krishna   One of the *avatars*, or incarnations of Vishnu. Hero of the *Mahabharata* epic.
Kubera   Lord of Wealth, Men and Genii. Guardian of the North.
Kumbha   *Rakshasa* son of Kumbhakarna.
Kumbhakarna   *Rakshasa* brother of Ravana who attempts to kill Rama.
Kurma   King of tortoises, one of the *avatars* of Vishnu.

Lakshmana   One of Rama's brothers and his chief companion in his exile and battles.
Lakshmi   Wife of Vishnu, goddess of fortune.
Lanka   Kingdom ruled by Ravana.
Linga   'phallus', the symbol of Shiva. Adopted by the Khmer kings as the palladian of the kingdom.
Lokapalas   Guardians of the cardinal directions.
Lokeshvara   Another name for *Avalokiteshvara*, preferred by the Khmers.

Mahabharata   Indian epic.
Mahaparinirvana   Attainment of extinction of the self and cessation of the cycle of becoming.
Mahayana   The great vehicle school of Buddhism.
Mahendras   Mythological mountain at the centre of the Ocean.
Mahiparvata   A sacred mountain.
Mahout   The man who drives the elephant.
Makara   A sort of sea monster with the snout of an elephant and the body of a crocodile.
Mandapa   Antechamber, a pavilion in front of the main shrine.
Mandara   Mythological mountain of the gods, the king of mountains.
Mara   God who rules over the world of desire and enemy of the Buddha.
Marica   The demon that transformed into a deer/gazelle to distract Rama.

Mayavati   The reincarnation of Rati, the wife of Kama.

Meru, Mount   The mountain home of the gods.

Modaka   A sort of sweetmeat liked by Ganesha.

Mohodara   A *rakshasa* from the Battle of Lanka.

Muchalinda   The *naga*-king who sheltered the Buddha while he meditated.

Muka   A demon.

mukkuta   Conical head-dress worn by *asuras*.

Nagas   Water serpents who inhabit the oceans.

Nalgiri   Mad elephant sent to kill the Buddha by his jealous cousin.

Nandi   The sacred bull of Shiva.

Naraka   A demon slain by Indra.

Narantaka   One of Ravana's sons.

neak ta   Local deities associated with particular places.

Nikumba   *Rakshasa* son of Kumbhakarna.

Nila   The monkey general of Sugriva's army.

Nirrti   God of misery, guardian of the South-west.

Pandavas   The tribe who fought the Kauravas in the Battle of Kurukshetra.

Pandu   Father of Arjuna. Head of the Pandava tribe.

Parvati   Shiva's consort. Also known as Uma and Devi.

Phkak   Characteristic Khmer weapon, long-handled club with two blades inserted at an angle.

Phnom   Hill.

Prajñaparamita   The female version of the Bodhisattva.

Pradymna   Son of Krishna and Rukmini, the goddess of fortune.

Pralamba   A mystic mountain.

Prasada or *prasat*   Sanctuary tower.

Preah, *Prah*, *Pra*   Pertaining to anything sacred, holy.

Purohita   A family priest.

Rahu   Mythical demon said to cause eclipses of the sun or moon by eating it, assuming the shape of a meteor.

Rajahota   Royal priest.

Rajalalisatana   A way of sitting with one knee high, used mainly by princely people.

Rakshasas   Demon.

Rakshini   Female *rakshasa*.

Ramayana   Indian epic.

Rambha   A nymph with whom Viradha fell in love.

Ravana   The demon king of Lanka.

Rig Veda   Collection of sacrificial hymns dedicated to a pantheon of gods, composed from 1200 BC.

Rishi   A great sage or illuminated being.

Rudra   A Vedic god from the Rig Veda.

Sampati   The vulture brother of Jatayus.

Sampot   Short skirt around the waist, for men (*sarong* for women).

Samsara   The cycle of birth and rebirth.

Sarabhanga   Ascetic group visited by Rama, Sita, and Lakshmana.

Sarasvati   Spouse of Brahma.

Satyabhama   Wife of Garuda.

Satyavati   Step-mother of Bishma.

Shambara   The demon of drought, enemy of Indra.

Shastra   Indian architectural treatises.

Shiva   The auspicious one, god of ascetics, and of cosmic destruction and creation.

Shri (or *Sri*)   Vishnu's wife, Lakshmi.

Shuddhodama, King   Father of the future Buddha.

Shurpanakha   *Rakshini*, sister of Ravana.

Sita   The 'furrow', wife of Rama, daughter of Janaka.

Skanda   The god of war, son of Shiva.

Soma   God of the moon. Guardian of the Northeast.

Somasutra   Gargoyle, or spout, through which lustral water passes from the shrine to the outside.

Spean   Bridge.

Srah   Pond, water basin.

Srei   Woman.

Stung   River.

Sugriva   Monkey king, ally of Rama.

Sujata   Young girl who presented a gift to the Buddha before his enlightenment.

Sunda   *Asura* who fought with Upasand and caused havoc on earth.
Surya   Sun god, father of Sugriva.
Sushena   Monkey general, father of Tara, Valin's wife.
Swayamvara   A ceremony where a bride can choose her consort.

Tara   wife of Valin.
Tataka   *Rakshini* and mother of Marica.
Thom   Large, big.
Tilottama   Female divine being created by the gods to pacify two fighting *asuras* who were creasting havoc on earth.
Trijata   A *rakshini* who spoke in favour of Sita.
Trivikrama   Epithet of Vishnu when making three steps.

Uccaishrava   White horse of Indra produced from the Churning of the Ocean of Milk.
Uma   Daughter of the Himalayas, wife of Shiva. Also known as Parvati.
Upasunda   An *asura* who fought with Sunda.
Usha   Beautiful daughter of Bana.

Vahana   Mount or vehicle of a god.
Valin   King of the monkeys, son of Indra, brother of Sugriva, and husband of Tara.
Valmiki   Sage, composer of the *Ramayana*.
Varman   Protector.
Varuna   God of the ocean and guardian of the West.
Vasudeva   Father of Krishna.
Vasuki   Great king of the *nagas*.
Vayu   Guardian of the North West.
Vibhishana   Terrifying, *rakshasa* brother of Ravana, who left Lanka to join Rama.
Vihara   Rectangular building to house a Buddha image.
Vimana   Celestial palace of the gods.
Viradha   *Rakshasa* who attempted to abduct Sita.
Vishnu   The pervader, supreme god, the Maintainer of the Universe.
Vishvamita   A sage.

Wat (or *Vat*)   Temple.

Yaksha   Semi divine being, associated with Kubera.
Yama   King of the dead, sovereign over hell. Guardian of the South.
Yasoda   Krishna's adoptive mother.
Yuga   An age of the world.

Index

A

Agni 17, **46,** 92, 112, 114, 123

Airavata 21, 34, **35,** 42, 53, 54, **84,** 86, 108, 112, 124, **162,** 163

Amarendrapura 10

Amrita 54, 108, 146, **147**

Ananta 16, 17, 31, 42, **43,** 76

ancestor worship 14

Angada 126

Ang Chan, King 11, 112, 165

Angkor
abandonement of 11, 163
area 10, **78-79**
Conservancy 8, 15
Period 9, 14, 15, 16, 17, 18

Angkor Thom 11, 20, **21,** 66, 74, **80,** 160, 162

Angkor Wat 7, 10, 11, 12, 16, 20, 21, 22, 23, 24, 26, 80, 81, 85, 92, 98-99, **100,** 126, 145, 147, 151, 165, 166
plan 98-99
reliefs 17, **35, 37, 39-41,** **43, 45, 46, 55, 56, 58, 67,** 100-125, 141
style 162

Anidruddha 44, 46, 112

apsaras 22, 25, **26,** 54, **55,** 57, 75, 83, 90, 107, 108, 122, 123, 127, 128, 129, 134, 144, 145, 146, 148, 157, 163

Aranya Kanda 34

architecture, characteristics of 20, 71, 85

Arjuna **30,** 36, **52,** 86, **91,** 92, 94, 100, 101, 104, 122, 147

ark, sacred 148

army, Khmer 66, **67, 68-69,** 134, 135, 138, 148

Aryans 32

asceticism, cult of 50

ascetics 93, 112, 124, 127, 128, 129, 134, 140, 141, 142, 144, 145, 146, 147, 150, 152, **153**

ashramas 16

asuras 17, 21, 42, 44, **45,** 54, **56,** 57, 66, **82,** 90, 108, 113, 126, 144, 145, 146

Atlases 106, **107**

Austronesian language group 7

Avalokiteshvara 64, **65,** 148, **152,** 154, **166**

Aymonier, Etienne 8

Ayodhya 31, 32, 33, 34, 40, 90, 94, 123, 156

Ayutthaya 11, 12

B

Babhruvahavana 30

Bakheng 16

Bakong 10, 81, **82**

Baksei Chamkrong 10

Balaha 64, **65,** 154, 157, 158

Bala Kanda 33, 34, 85

Balarama 46, 57, 85, 112, 118

Bali, King 42, 44

Bana 44, **45,** 46, 57, 97, 112

Banteay Chhmar 11, 59, 81, **152-153**

Banteay Kdei 11, 59, 79, 81, **155**

Banteay Samre 11, 15, 16, **46,** 60, **126-131**

Banteay Srei 10, **14,** 15, **35,** 36, **37, 39, 45, 49, 51,** 52, **53,** **56, 58,** 81, **83-91,** 147

Bapuon 10, 12, 16, 23, 24, 36, **39, 40,** 42, **45, 52,** 80, 81, 92, **93-96**

barays 10, 11, 10, 97

Bastian, Adolf 8

battles 11, 21, 24, 30, 33, 44-47, 57, **68-71, 82,** 101-**105,** 112-117, 140
Devas and *Asuras* 113
of Lanka **39,** 114-117
Krishna and *Asuras* 112
Vishnu and *Asuras* 112
with Chams 57, 68-70

Bayon 11, 18, 19, 20, 21, 22, 24, **25, 26,** 59, 79-81, 83, 104, **131-150**
Inner gallery 25, **26,** 48, 51, 141-150
Outer gallery **25,** 57, 66, **67-71,** 134-140
period 163, 164
style 155, 165

Beng Mealea 11

Bhagavad Gita 30, 57, 104

Bhagavad Purana 29, 42, 44, 54, 76, 85, 92, 93, 108, 118, 123

Bhima 57, **58,** 90

birds **81**

Bishma 30, 57, **58,** 92, 101

boar 50, 52

boats 148, 157

Bodhisattvas **18,** 30, 131, **152,** 154, **158-159,** 162

Boisselier, Jean 66

Borobudur 104

Bosch, Frederik D. K. 148

Brah Dharani 166

Brahma 15, 17, 34, **35,** 42, 50, 59, 86, **87,** 97, 114, 118, 127, **128, 140,** 146, **147,** 152, **153,** 163

Brahmanda Purana 50, 118

Brahmins 9, 14, 15, 19, 21, 22, 50, 66, 75, 85, 104, **105,** 118, 142, 144, 145

Buddha, the   60, *see also*
    Buddha images
Buddha images   18, 59-65, 148,
    156-165
    and *Naga*-king   160
    and elephant Nalgiri   **65,**
    161
    and Sujata   161
    attaining *nirvana*   **65,** 161
    bhumisparsa mudra   **163**
    blessing family   161, **162**
    cutting of hair   61, 157, 158
    destruction of   18, 151,
    155, **156,** 157
    Great Departure of   60, **61,**
    151, 158, 165
    in meditation   62, **63,** 156,
    157, 158, 161, 162
    reclining   **65**
    reliefs   59-65
    seated under *naga*   **18, 59,**
    62
    standing   **161**
Buddharaja   19
Buddhacarita   29
Buddhavamsa   29
Buddhism   8, 10, 14, 151
    Mahayana   11, 14, 17, 18,
    54, 60, 131, 155, 165
    Tantric   18, 60
    Theravada   14, 18-19, 59,
    60, 160, 163, 165
Buddhist myths   29, 59-65, 131,
    151-152, 155-167
Buffalo   54, **55,** 114
buffalo sacrifice   134-**135**
Burma   7, 11, 14

C
Cardamom mountains   7
caste   9
Ceylon, *see* Sri Lanka
Chakravartin   19
chameleon   50
Champa   11
Chams   11, 18, 21, 33, 57
    battles with   57, **68-69, 70,**
    134, 138, 140, 142

Chandaka   60, **61,** 164
Chau Say Tevoda   11, 79, 81,
    130
Chenla   9
China   8, 75
Chinese
    style   12, 112-**113,** 164
    travellers, *see also* Zhou
    Daguan   7, 134
    texts   8
Chitralekha   44
Churning of the Ocean of Milk
    16, **17,** 29, 44, 54, **55,** 59,
    76, 97, 108, **110-111,** 118,
    125, 127, **128,** 145, **147,**
    162, 163, **167**
Citragupta   54, **55,** 106
Cœdès, George   22, 138, 140,
    144, 147
clown   106
cremations   23, 145, 146
crocodile   17, 134

D
Dagens, Bruno   97
daily life scenes, *see* reliefs
dancing girl   86, **90**
Dandaka forest   34
Dangrek mountains   7, 10
Dasharatha, King   30, 31
deer   140, **141**
de Lagrée, Douart   8
de Lajonquière, Lunet   8, 97
Delaporte, Louis   8
de Remusat, Coral   23
Devadatta   64
Devaki   42
Devaraja concept   9, 15, 19
Devarata, King   34
Devas   54, 57, 66, 108, 113,
    114, 145
devatas   22, 25, 75, **76**
Devi, *see* Uma
Dharanindravarman II   160
Dharmasamhita   50
Dharmma   54, **55,** 106
Dhritarashtra   57
dragons   17

Draupadi   122
Dravidian tribes   32
Dumont, René   20
Durga   15, 86, **90**
Duryodhama   57, **58,** 90
dvarapala figures   **83, 91,** 146
Dvaravati water festival   122,
    145

E
East Baray   10
East Mebon   10
Ecole Française d' Extrême
    Orient (EFEO)   8, 81, 92
elephants   65, **67-70,** 71, 94,
    105, 115, **117,** 134, 138,
    139, 140, 154, 161, **162**
Elephant range   7
Elephant Terrace   11, **74,** 80,
    81, 154
Europeans   7

F
face towers   21, 131, **133, 155**
festivals   122, 145
Fine Arts Department, Phnom
    Penh   8
fish   138, 140, **141,** 142
fishing   138
'flying palaces'   22, 94
'freeing the woman legend'
    148, **149**
French   19, 81
Funan   8, 9

G
Ganapati, *see* Ganesha
Ganesha   17, 112, 146
Ganga   146
Garnier, Francis   8
Garuda   16, 22, 44, **45,** 46, **47,**
    75, 76, **77,** 94, **96,** 106, **107,**
    112, 124, 142, **143, 154**
Giteau, Madelaine   164, 165,
    166

Glaize, Maurice   22, 50, 81, 118, 141, 160, 162
Goldman, Robert P.   30
Goloubew, Victor   85
Great Lake, the, *see* Tonlé Sap
Grison, Pierre   20
Groslier, Bernard P.   83
Groslier, George   97
Guardian figures   21
guru   83

H

hamsa   **35,** 50, **95,** 1144, 148, 152, **153**
Hanuman   32, 33, 38, **39,** 92, 94, **96,** 108, 115, **116,** 122, 123, 145
Harihara   17
Hariharalaya   10
Harivamsa   29, 42, 118
Harivamsha   85, 112
Heavens and Hells reliefs   22, 24, 54, 55, 56, 106, 107
   Heavens   107
   Hells   106, 108, **109**
Hevajra   18
Himalayas   7, 19
Hinduism   8, 15, 17, 18
Hirangakashipu, King   90, **91**
Historical procession   66, **67,** 104, **105,** 106, 134
horse-headed god   86, **91**
horses   **101**
horsemen   **157**
hospitals   11, 59
hunting scenes   **74**
hydraulic engineering   19

I

Iliad, the   29
India and Indian influence   8, 9, 14, 66, 75, 83, 104
   cosmology   20
   epics   21, 29
   mythology   24
   religion, *see* Buddhism and Hinduism

script, *see* Sanskrit
   trade with   8
   treatises   20
indigenous deities   14
Indonesia   66, 75, 104, 124
Indra   21, 22, 34, **35,** 36, 42, 46, 52, **53,** 54, 62, 66, **84,** 85, 86, 97, 108, 114, 118, 122, 123, 124, 140, 141, 161
   rain of   **53, 84,** 85, 127
Indrabhisaka   140
Indradevi, Queen   25
Indrajit   32, 38, **40, 41,** 94, 125, 126
Indrapura   10
Indratataka   10
Indravarman I, King   10, 82
inscriptions   8, 9, 16, 21

J

Jacques, Claude   23
Janaka, King   31, 34, 122
Japanese   8
Jatakas   29
Jatayus   31
Java   9
Javanese art   81, 82
Jayadevi, Queen   25
Jayatataka baray   11
Jayavarman II, King   9, 10, 15, 19
Jayavarman IV, King   10
Jayavarman V, King   10, 83
Jayavarman VII, King   11, 17, 18, 21, 22, **25,** 33, 57, 59, 60, 64, 66, 74, 97, 131, 151, 152, 154, 157, 158, 160
Jayavarman VIII, King   11, 131, 160

K

Kabhanda   31, 36, **37,** 122, 124
Kailasa Mountain, *see* Mount Kailasa
kalas   75, **76-77**
Kalanemi   37, 114
Kalidasa   86

Kalindi river   44
Kaliya   44, **45**
Kama   50, **51,** 85, **87,** 118, 142, 146
Kamsa   42, 44, **45,** 85-87, **92-93**
Kanthaka   60, **61,** 62, 164, 165
Karandavyu Sutra   64
Kaundinya   26, 125
Kauravas   29, 30, 57, 92, **101**
Kbal Spean   50
Ketu   123
Khmer civilization   7, 8
   language   7, 9
   society, *see* Women in Khmer society
kings   **105, 135, 149, 150,**
kinnaras   126
kinnari   112
kingship   9, 12-13, 66, 71, 104,
kirata   52
Koh Ker   10, 20
Kishkindha Kanda   38
Kompong Cham   12, 165
Kravan, Prasat   **16**
Krishna   16, 17, 29, **30,** 42, 43, 44, **45-47,** 57, **58, 84,** 85, **89,** 97, 112, **113,** 118, 122, 123, 124
   fighting lion and elephant   97
   fighting Kaliya   44, **45,** 127
   infancy of   92, **93**
   killing Kamsa   **45,** 85, 86-87
   Krishna Govardhanadhara   16, **46,** 127, 151
   Victory over Bana   164, **165**
Kubera   34, 36, 42, 53, 97, 114, 123
Kulen, Mount   10
Kumarasambhava   52, 86
Kumba   115, **117**
Kumbhakarna   38, **39,** 94, **95,** 115
Kumbhanda   154
Kurma   **17,** 54, 127, **128**
Kurukshetra, Battle of   24, 29, 30, 57, **58,** 90, 92, 96, 100-**105**

L

Lakshmana 31, 32, 34, 36, **37**, 38, **39-41**, 86, 94-**96, 115, 116,** 122, 123, 124, 125, 126
Lakshmi 16, 54, 123, 148
Lalitavistara 29
Lanka, Battle of 32, 33, 38, 40, 57, 94, 114-**117**, 126, 151
Lanka, Isle of 64
Lanka, Kingdom of 31
Laos 7, 8, 10, 11
Le Bonheur, Albert 23, 90, 108, 112, 124
Leper King 148, **149, 150**
Leper King, Terrace of 11, 80, 81, **154**
'libraries' 20, 83, 128
linga 10, 15, **19,** 50, 51, 83, 134, 148, 164
lions **35,** 86, 114, 123
lizard 50, 141, 146
Lokeshvara **18,** 59, 64, **65,** 131, **157, 158-159**
Lolei inscription **9**
Lolei temple 10
Loy Kratong festival 122

M

Mahabharata 24, 29, 30, 42-50, 53, 54, 57, 90, 92, 94, 122, 147
Mahayana, see Buddhism
Mahendraparvata 10
Maheshvara 92
Mahiparvata, Mountain 46
mahout 104, **105**
makaras 75, **77, 88,** 97
Malay peninsula 11
Manasura 20
Mangalartha 17
maps 6, 78-81
Mara 62, **63**
Marchal, Henri 160
Marica **31,** 36, 118
marine creatures 108
matrilineal descent 24-25
Mayamata 20
Mayavati 142-144

Mekong river 7
missionaries 7
Mohodara 115
Mongols 11
monkeys 93, 94, **95-96,** 114, **115-116,** 118-**121,** 123, **126,** 134
monsoon climate 7
moon god 127, **129,** 146
Mouhot, Henri 7, 26
Mount Govardhana 118
Mount Kailasa 31, 34, **35,** 118, 126, 147
Mount Mahaparvata 124
Mount Malaya 36, 94, 124
Mount Mandara 54, 108
Mount Meru 19, 21, 22, 59, 124, 142
Muang Tam **76**
Muchalinda **59,** 62, 76
Muka 52, 92, 147
Musée Guimet 56, 90
musicians **129**

N

nagas 17, 21, 42, 44, **45,** 75-**77,** 85, 108, 110, 114, 145, **149, 154,** 164
naga bridge 59, 160
naga king 146, **147**
naga princess 125
Nalgiri 64, **65**
Nandi, the bull 15, 22, 85, **87,** 97, 146
Naraka 124
Narantaka 46, 115, **117**
narrative techniques 24
nats 14
naval battles **70,** 134, 138
Neak Pean 11, **18,** 59, 64, **65,** 79, 81, **158-159**
neak ta 14
Nikhumha 115, **116**
Nila 115, **119**
Nirrti 34, 86, 123

O

Odyssey, the 29

P

Pagan 11
Pancarata sect 16
Pandavas 29, 57, 90, **102-103,** 104
Pandu 52
Paramavishnuloka, *see* Suryavarman II
Paramaraja I, King 12, 112
Parilyyaka Forest 62, **65,** 161
Paris, Philippe 20
Parmentier, Henri 165
Parvati, *see also* Uma 52, 112
Pashupta 147
peacock 34, **35,** 114
phallus, *see linga*
Phimai 11, 59
Phimeanakas inscription 21
Phimeanakas temple 10
Phnom Bakheng 10, 12, 22
Phnom Bok 10
Phnom Chisor 10, 81, **97**
Phnom Da Vishnu 16
Phnom Kbal Spean 141
Phnom Krom 10
Phnom Kulen 12, 141
Phnom Penh 7
Phnom Penh National Museum 60, 90
Phnom Rung 23
Pichard 23
polo players **74,** 154
Post-Angkorean period 18
Pradyumna 112, 142-**143**
Prahasta 115, **119**
Prajñaparamita 18, 59
Pralamba 118, **119**
Prambanan 124
Prasat Khna Sen Kev 10
Prasat Komnap 16
Prasat Kravan **4, 16,** 17
Prasat Trapeang Run 16
Preah Khan 11, 18, 38, 42, **43,** 46, 59, 79, 81, **151**
Preah Khan at Kompong Svay 11, 59

Preah Ko 10
Preah Palilay 10, **63, 65,** 77, 80, 81, **160-162**
Preah Pithu 10, 12, 15, 16, **43,** 80, 81, 160, **162-164**
Preah Vihear 10, 77
pre-Angkorean period 9, 15, 16, 17, 20, 22
Preau Cruciform 124-125
Pre Rup temple 10, 20
princesses 104, **105,** 134, **135,** 142, 144, 145, 148
processions 145, 146, 148
Puranas 29, 42, 50, 52
Purusottama 16
Pushpaka chariot 32, 92, 94, **95,** 122

R
Rahu 75, 108, 146, 152, **153**
rajahota 104, 106-**107**
Rajendravarman, King 10, 83
rakshasa 94, **95,** 115, **117, 119,** 122, 126, 127
rakshini 64
Rama 10, 16, 29, 30, 31, 32, 33, 34, 36, **37,** 38, **39,** 40, 42, 115, **116,** 118, **121,** 122, 123, 124, **130**
    and Sita 155, **156**
    on Hanuman **126**
Ramakien 30, 31
Ramakerti 31, 38
Ramayana 16, 24, 29, 30-41, 53, 57, 85, 86, 92, 93, 94, 96, 106, 115, 118, 122, 123, 124, 126, 130, **151, 156**
Rati 118, 146
Ravana **28,** 31, 32, 33, 36, 38, 50, 94, 96, 115, **116,** 118, 122, 123, 125, 126, 141
    abducting Sita **28,** 90
    shaking Mt. Kailasa 34-**35,** 85, 86, **130,** 147
Ravananugraha murti 86
Reamker 31
relief subject matter
    battle scenes 57, **58, 68-71, 101-103, 105, 115**

Buddhist scenes **59-65, 151, 152, 156,-159, 161-164, 166**
daily life scenes 24, **25,** 66, 71, **72-74,** 92, **95,** 131, **136-137,** 138, **139**
historical scenes 24, **67, 70-71, 105,** 107, 139
Mahabharata scenes 24, **30, 43,** 45-47, 52, 56, 58
Ramayana scenes 24, **28, 31, 35, 37, 39, 41, 87-89, 91 95, 96, 115-117, 119-121, 123, 125, 126, 130, 151, 156, 167**
royal scenes **25, 26** 105, **107, 134, 135,** 138, 140, 142, 145, 146
symbolism of 23
religion *see* Buddhism, Hinduism
rest houses 11
rhinoceros 17, **46,** 112, 114, 123
Richman, Paula 29
Rig Vedas 50, 53
rituals 14, 21, 22
Roluos 10, 82
Rong Chen 10
Royal Palace 154, 160
    ponds 154, **155**
Royal Terrace 22
Rudra 50

S
Sakyamuni Buddha 18
Sambor Prei Kuk 22, 81
Sampati 32
sanctuary towers 148, **149**
Sangada 115, **117**
Sanskrit 8, 9, 14, 21, 22
Santanu 57
Sarasvati 17
Satyabhama 124
Satyavati 57
Saura Purana 50
Shaiva sect 15
Shiva 10, 14, 15, 16, 17, 34, **35,** 36, **37,** 42, 44, **45,** 40-**52,**

59, 83, 85-86, **87,** 92, 94, 112, **113,** 114, 118, 122, 142, 144, **145,** 148, 163
Bhikshatana murti 50, 118, **119, 141,** 146
dancing **14,** 15, **91, 97,** 146, 163
disturbed by Ravana **130**
fighting Arjuna 86, **91**
in meditation 15, 85, 122
on Nandi 86, 90, **91,** 97, 130, 146, **147**
with Kama 85, 87, 118, 146
with Uma 15, **35, 49,** 50-**52,** 54, **55,** 85-87, **90-91,** 97, 118, 127, **129,** 130, 146, **147**
Shivaism 15, 18
Shivalinga 97
Shiva Purana 50
Shridrakumara 152
Shuddodama, King 60
Shurpanakha 31, 33
Siamese 11, 66, 106, **107**
Siddha 118
Siddhartha Gautama 29
Siem Reap 7
Simhala 64
Sita 31, 32, 33, 34, 36, 38, **39,** 86, 115, 118, **123, 130**
    abduction by Ravana **28,** 36, 90
    abduction by Viradha 34, 36, **37**
    ordeal of 32, 33, **40,** 92
    with Hanuman **39,** 93, 94, 122
Skanda 34, **35,** 42, 86, 114, 123, 126, 128, **129**
slaves 9
'Sleep of Women' 60, **61,** 165
soldiers **23, 67-69**
Soma (moon god) 34
Soma (*naga*-princess) 75
somasutra 145
Srah Srang 10, **77**
Sri Lanka 64
Sudharma 20
Sugriva 32, 38, **39, 41,** 54, 86, **88,** 90, 94, 96, 108, 115,

117, 118, 123, 124, **130,** 164
Sujata   62, **63**
Sun god   146
Sunda   **56,** 90
Sundara Kanda   38
Suor Prat, Prasats   80
Surya   17, 34, **35,** 42, 53, 114,
   127, **129,** 154
Suryaparvata   97
Suryavarman I, King   10, 18,
   97, 100
Suryavarman II, King   10-**11,**
   22, 66, 100, 104, 108
Sushena   32, 38, 125, 126
Svayamvara of Sita   122

T
Ta Keo   10
Ta Nei   59, 81, **157**
Ta Prohm   11, 18, 59, 79, 81,
   151
Ta Prohm of Bati   **65,** 81, **167**
Ta Som   59
tantric concepts   11, 18
Tara   32, 38, 118, **120-121,** 122,
   125, **130,** 148
Tataka   31, 36, 91
Ta Tout   163
temple-mountains   10, 19
temple plans   **20**
Tep Pranam   59, 80, 160, 162
Terrace of the Elephants, *see*
   Elephant Terrace
Thailand, Gulf of   8
Thais   11, 31
Thai style   163, **164**
Theravada, *see* Buddhism
Thommanon   11, 79, 81, **130**
Thomson, John   8
Tibet   7
Tilottama   **56,** 90
Tonlé Sap lake   7
Tonlé Sap region   9
Tonlé Sap river   7
tortures   106, 107-**108**
Tribhuvanamahesvara   83
Trijata   122
turtle   16, 17, 54, **55,** 108, **162,**
   163

U
Uccaishrava   54, 108, 163
Udayadityavarman II, King   10,
   92
Uma   15, 16, **49,** 50, **51, 55,** 85,
   86, **87,** 146, **147**
UNESCO   8
Upansunda   **56,** 90
Usha   44, 46
Uttara Kanda   33, 34, 40

V
Valin   32, 36, 38, **41,** 86, 88,
   90, 94, 96, 118, **120-121,**
   122, 125, **130,** 164
Valmiki   31, 32, 34, 36, 38,
   114, 118, 122
Vamana   42
Varuna   34, **35,** 42, 53, 114,
   123
Vasuki   54, 76, 108, **110,** 163
Vat Nagar, *see* Wat Nokor
Vedas   52, 53
Vedic tradition   140
Vessantara Jataka   29 127, 162
Vibhishana   38, 108, **110,** 115,
   116, 122, 123
Vidhura   162
Vidhurapandita Jataka   162
Vidyadhara   118
Vientiane   11
Vietnam   7
Viradha   31, 34, 36, **37,** 86,
   123, 124
Vishnu   **4,** 10, 15, 16, 17, 29,
   31, 33, 34, 42, 43, **48,** 50,
   54, 76, 90, **91,** 93, 97, 100,
   108, 114, 122, 123, 126,
   127, 128, 130, 144, **145,**
   146, **147,** 148, 151, 163
   anantasayin   16, 42, **43,** 76,
   97, 125, **128,** 151
   narasimha   90, **91**
   nataraja   17
   on garuda   **16,** 42, **43,** 44,
   47, 86, 100, 112, 127, 130,
   144, 163, 164
   trivikrama   16, 17, 42, **43,**
   97, 125, 127 (trivikrana)

victory over *Asuras*   112,
   125
   victory over Bana   112
Vishnuism   10, 12, 15, 16
Vishnukumara   83
Vishvamita   36
Vizajaya   **67**

W
Wat Baray   10
Wat Ek   10
Wat Eng Khna   50, **51**
Wat Nokor   12, 60, **61, 63,** 76-
   77, 81, 164, **165-166**
Wat Phu   10
water festival   145 (*see also*
   Dvarati water festival)
West Baray   10
West Mebon   10
women, role of   24-25
World Heritage Site   8

Y
Yaksa   118
yakshas   21
Yama   34, **37,** 42, 53, 54, **55,**
   86, 106, 114, 123, 126
Yanjnavaraha   83
Yashoda   44, 118
Yashodharapura   97
Yashovarman I, King   10, 16,
   59, 160
yogic practices   15
Yuddha Kanda   38, 125

Z
Zhou Daguan   7, 11, 15, 26, 71